Christ Our Life

We Believe

Authors

Sisters of Notre Dame
Chardon, Ohio

Reviewers

Sister Mary Judith Bucco, S.N.D.

Sister Margaret Mary Friel, S.N.D.

Sister Mary Jean Hoelke, S.N.D.

Sister Mary Cordell Kopec, S.N.D.

Sister Mary Charlotte Manzo, S.N.D.

Sister Ann Mary McLaughlin, S.N.D.

Sister Mary Donnalee Resar, S.N.D.

Sister Katherine Mary Skrabec, S.N.D.

Sister Eileen Marie Skutt, S.N.D.

Sister Mary Jane Vovk, S.N.D.

LOYOLAPRESS.

CHICAGO

Nihil Obstat
Reverend John G. Lodge, S.S.L., S.T.D.
Censor Deputatus
May 22, 2007

Imprimatur
Reverend John F. Canary, S.T.L., D.Min.
Vicar General, Archdiocese of Chicago
May 25, 2007

Christ Our Life
found to be in conformity

The *Nihil Obstat* and *Imprimatur* are official declarations that a book is free of doctrinal and moral error. No implication is contained therein that those who have granted the *Nihil Obstat* and *Imprimatur* agree with the content, opinions, or statements expressed. Nor do they assume any legal responsibility associated with publication.

The Ad Hoc Committee to Oversee the Use of the Catechism, United States Conference of Catholic Bishops, has found the doctrinal content of this catechetical series, copyright 2009, to be in conformity with the *Catechism of the Catholic Church.*

Acknowledgments

Excerpts from the *New American Bible* with Revised New Testament and Psalms Copyright © 1991, 1986, 1970 Confraternity of Christian Doctrine, Inc., Washington, DC. All rights reserved. No portion of the *New American Bible* may be reprinted without permission in writing from the copyright holder.

Excerpts from the English translation of *The Roman Missal* © 1973, International Committee on English in the Liturgy, Inc. (ICEL); excerpts from English translation of *Rite of Penance* © 1974, ICEL; excerpts from the English translation of *A Book of Prayers* © 1982, ICEL; excerpts from the English translation of *A Book of Blessings* © 1988, ICEL. All rights reserved.

Excerpts from *Catechism of the Catholic Church*. English translation of the *Catechism of the Catholic Church* for the United States of America copyright © 1994, United States Catholic Conference, Inc.—Libreria Editrice Vaticana.

English translation of the Apostles' Creed and the Nicene Creed by the International Consultation on English texts.

Loyola Press has made every effort to locate the copyright holders for the cited works used in this publication and to make full acknowledgment for their use. In the case of any omissions, the publisher will be pleased to make suitable acknowledgments in future editions.

Cover art: Lori Lohstoeter
Cover design: Loyola Press and Think Design Group
Interior design: Think Design Group and Kathryn Seckman Kirsch, Loyola Press

ISBN 13: 978-0-8294-2410-2, ISBN 10: 0-8294-2410-5

© 2009 Loyola Press and Sisters of Notre Dame, Chardon, Ohio

Dedicated to St. Julie Billiart, foundress of the Sisters of Notre Dame, in gratitude for her inspiration and example

LOYOLAPRESS.

3441 N. ASHLAND AVENUE
CHICAGO, ILLINOIS 60657
(800) 621-1008
www.ChristOurLife.org
www.LoyolaPress.org

Printed in the United States of America.

07 08 09 10 11 12 13 14 15 Web 10 9 8 7 6 5 4 3 2 1

Contents

Especially for Families

A Note to Families begins on page v. There is a Letter Home at the beginning of each unit. At the end of each unit, you will find a Family Feature that explores ways to nurture faith at home.

(continued next page)

iii

(continued from previous page)

Note to Families

How you can nurture your child's faith

This is an important year in your child's spiritual development. The *We Believe* text is designed to help your child learn that God calls each one of us to faith and eternal life with him as members of the faith community, the Church.

The focus of this year's study is faith, which is belief and trust in a God who knows us, loves us, and calls us by name. The children will become familiar with the mysteries of faith that we profess in the Apostles' Creed. Through events from both the Old and the New Testaments of the Bible, they will learn of God's saving love for his people and the truths of our faith. The goal is for your child to respond with a trusting, joyful relationship with God and to accept all that God has taught us.

Features designed specifically for families

Because the way you live your faith as a family has a profound impact on your child, the Christ Our Life series provides Building Family Faith features at the end of most chapters. Typically, a chapter is presented in class each week. Building Family Faith activities provide an opportunity for you to review the material with your child and to share your response to these elements of our faith. Each Building Family Faith is composed of five sections:

Chapter Summary provides a brief overview of the concepts covered in the chapter.

Reflect cites a short selection from Scripture that reflects the theme of the chapter.

Discuss as a Family provides questions to help you apply the Scripture reading to daily life.

Pray sums up the message for the week in a short prayer that everyone can pray daily. This prayer can be printed and posted on the refrigerator, bathroom mirror, or on a stand-up card on your kitchen table. You may add it to meal prayers or to other family prayers.

Do provides ideas for sharing at meals and for other family activities related to the message of the chapter. Be sure to review all the suggestions and select the ones that most appeal to you or seem particularly worthwhile for your family. Feel free to brainstorm other ideas among your family members.

Note to Families

Remember, the Building Family Faith activities are only suggestions. Please feel free to adapt them or to develop some ideas of your own. But be sure to have regular discussions with your child about faith. As you talk to your child about God, you help the roots of his or her faith grow deeper.

Finally, you can use the We Remember section at the end of each chapter to help your child master the concepts covered in each chapter.

The Lessons Your Child Will Learn

The year begins with the lesson that we are called to be God's holy people. Your child will also learn that the gifts and talents we receive from God are part of what makes each of us unique and that we are meant to use those gifts and talents for the good of all.

Next the children learn that God is powerful, loving, holy, just, merciful, and good. They learn to love and respect God and desire to be closer to him. God wants good things for his children, and his plan is rooted in love. The lesson includes a description of how God showed his abiding love by sending his son, Jesus, to live among us and reveal the Kingdom of God, which is a kingdom of love.

The children will also learn the story of Jesus: how he was sent by God to save us and was faithful to God's plan, even in the face of a brutal death. The children will learn that Jesus rose on the third day and that his Resurrection is a victory over death, sin, and despair. Through his rising, we belong to the Kingdom of God along with the saints in heaven. After Jesus ascended into heaven, he sent his Holy Spirit to protect and guide the Church.

Though Jesus ascended into heaven, we celebrate his presence through the sacraments, which help us answer our call to be holy. The children learn that God longs to forgive us and that he gave us the Sacrament of Penance and Reconciliation. He also longs to feed and strengthen our faith through the Sacrament of the Eucharist. By the gift of the sacraments, God shares the wondrous life of grace, and through his grace we can find our true happiness and satisfaction.

Visit **www.ChristOurLife.org/family** for more family resources.

God Calls Us to Faith

I have called you by name: you are mine.

Isaiah 43:1

A Letter Home

Dear Parents and Family,

Welcome! This year and this program present a wonderful opportunity for you to embark with your child on a discovery of what Catholics believe. Engaging with your child's studies at home will help make this learning relevant for your child and demonstrate its importance in your own life.

The third-grade program of *Christ Our Life* presents the main truths of Catholicism as expressed in the Apostles' Creed. The children will study God as he is revealed in creation, in his interaction with his Chosen People, and in the life and teachings of Jesus Christ. They will see that they are called to be part of God's holy people in the community of the Church.

The children are first introduced to people who serve as models of fidelity to God's call. Through these stories, the children are reminded that they, too, are called by God to be his holy people. They play a part in Jesus' mission of leading all people to God.

The children are introduced to Abraham and to Ruth as models of holy people who said yes to God even when it was challenging. Chapter 2 presents King David, and the children learn how he used his talents and gifts from God. The children are encouraged to develop their own gifts to help others and to praise and glorify God.

The third chapter is about Jesus, who is the Way, the Truth, and the Life. The children will learn how Jesus shows us the one true way to a life in friendship with God. In the fourth chapter, the children will learn about Mary, the Mother of God. Mary's heroic yes encourages the children to respond willingly to God and to trust him, just as she courageously did.

The final chapter features Jesus' call to the apostles, to the disciples, and to Paul. The stories of these ordinary people and their extraordinary response to God's call show the children that they can proclaim Jesus' message even in the small things they do each day.

At the end of each chapter in this unit, the children will bring home a review of the chapter along with the Building Family Faith feature, which will give you a quick review of what your child has learned. At the end of the unit, the children will bring home the Family Feature handout to help nurture the family's faith at home.

Visit **www.ChristOurLife.org/family** for more family resources.

God Calls Us

God Calls Us by Name

"Hi, Marty!" "Tina!" "Mario!" Excited voices rang out as friends greeted each other after vacation.

Leah felt strange and alone. No one called her name. No one knew her. Then she heard "Leah!" and looked up. Miss Link called out, "Boys and girls, this is Leah Suh. She's in our class this year. Leah has come from Miami, Florida."

"Hi, Leah!" "Welcome, Leah!" children called from all parts of the room. Leah smiled as she looked around. Everyone called her by name. Now she "belonged."

- When have you felt strange and alone? How do you feel when someone calls you by name?
- What makes you feel you "belong"?

We Are Family

You belong to your family at home. When you were baptized, you joined another family, the Catholic Church. You also belong to the big Christian family of all people who believe in Jesus.

You have two special names that show that you belong to the family of Jesus. Now you are called a Christian and a Catholic.

You also belong to the great human family of people all over the world.

All these families belong to God.

A Message from God

Write the letter that comes after the given one. Find out what God says to us.

"I will be your <u>G O D</u> , and you
 F N C

will be my <u>P E O P L E</u> ."
 O D N O K D

Leviticus 26:12

God Speaks to Us in the Bible

God wants us to get to know him. He speaks to us in our hearts and through the Bible. The Bible is filled with stories of how God speaks to his people and how people respond to God in faith.

God Called Abram to Believe

A long time ago God called a man named Abram. God said, "Leave your home and your country. Go to the land I will show you. I will make of you a great nation."

Abram believed that God would take care of him. He did as God told him. He went to the new land.

Then God spoke to Abram again. He gave him the land and said, "Look up at the sky. Count the stars if you can. The children of your family will be as many as the stars in the sky. You shall be called Abraham, and your wife shall be called Sarah. You and Sarah will have a son."

Abraham believed what God said. Although he and Sarah were very old, they had a son. They called him Isaac. He was a great joy to them.

God Gives the Gift of Faith

Abraham always believed in God's loving care. He did what God asked even when it was hard. Even though we cannot see God, he also calls us to believe him.

At Baptism we celebrate the gift of faith. It helps us believe in God. We believe that God made us and that we are his children. We believe that God takes care of us in everything that happens. We believe that we can live with him forever.

Just as God spoke to Abraham, he speaks to us in our hearts. He helps us know him better. He helps us do what he tells us even when it is hard. With faith we trust God to do what is good for us. We know God wants us to be happy.

God Called Ruth to Believe

The Book of Ruth is about a young woman named Ruth. Ruth was from Moab, a country where people believed in false gods. She learned about the one true God from her husband and his mother, Naomi. When her husband died, Ruth stayed with Naomi. Naomi was kind and Ruth loved her.

One day Naomi decided to go back to Bethlehem, the city in Israel where she had been born. Ruth wanted to go with her. She said to Naomi:

> "Wherever you go, I will go.
> Where you live, I will live.
> Your people shall be my people,
> and your God my God."
>
> adapted from Ruth 1:16

Ruth went with Naomi to Israel. In the new country she worked hard every day. She gathered grain in the fields of a man named Boaz.

Boaz was good and kind. Before long, he married Ruth. They were very happy together. God blessed them with a son. Ruth became the great-grandmother of King David. Into the family of David, many years later, Jesus the Savior was born.

God called Ruth to believe in him. She learned about God from Naomi and the Israelites. God was pleased with Ruth and gave her the gift of faith. Ruth knew God and loved him.

God Calls You to Believe

Abraham and Ruth had faith in God. They knew and loved God. You received the gift of faith at Baptism when you became a Christian. What things do you do that please God?

Write the names of people who help you learn about God.

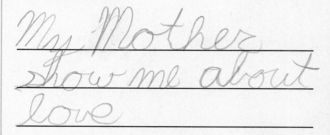

Mis. M
the Priest
Our Parents

Write what you learned about God from one of them.

My Mother
show me about
love

A Moment with Jesus

Imagine getting a phone call from Jesus. What do you say when you get on the phone with Jesus? Let him know that you are always ready to answer his call.

A Picture from Your Life

Draw a picture of your family.

When you were baptized, you joined the Church and the family of Jesus. Since then, you have had two special names that mean that you belong to the Church family. What are they?

Your Special Names

Print these names in the puzzle.

A cross-shaped crossword puzzle with the words:
C A T H O L I C (across)
C H R I S T I A S (down)

We Remember

What does God call us to do?
God calls us to believe in him and to do what he asks.

What is faith?
Faith is a gift from God that helps us to believe in him.

We Respond

I know that God is with me.
In God I trust.

adapted from Psalm 56:10,12

Building Family Faith

CHAPTER SUMMARY God calls us to take part in his plan of salvation. He promises to help and bless all those who trustingly respond to his call. Abraham and Ruth show us how. They show us that having faith means listening for and obeying what God asks. They exemplify how faithfulness to God is good and proper and leads to a fuller, richer life.

REFLECT
Fear not, for I have redeemed you;
    I have called you by name: you are mine.
                                Isaiah 43:1

DISCUSS AS A FAMILY
• What does this reading tell us about God's love?
• What good things can you name that God has given your family?
• How do you show your faithfulness to God in the way you live as a family?

PRAY
I have called you by name: you are mine.

DO
• Learn the meaning of each family member's name.
• Make a photo collage of your family. Print the words of Isaiah 43:1 around it.
• Ask your child to tell you the stories of Abraham and Ruth answering God's call.
• Make a connection between these stories and your family's experiences.

Visit **www.ChristOurLife.org/family** for more family resources.

God Gives Us Gifts

God Calls Us to Use Our Gifts

God has a plan to form a people of his own. God's plan includes us too. He calls us to believe in him and to lead other people to know and love him. We can help God carry out his plan by using the gifts and special abilities he has given us.

The Parable of the Talents

One day a man was going on a journey. Before he left, he called his servants together. He gave each one some money, called talents, to take care of. To one he gave five talents. To another he gave two talents. To a third he gave one talent. The first two servants used their talents wisely. The one with five talents used them to earn another five, and the one with two earned another two. But the third servant was afraid of losing what the man had given him, so he buried his one talent in the ground.

When the man returned, he praised the first two servants because they had doubled the money he had given them. He said, "Well done, my good and faithful servants. Since you were faithful in small matters, I will give you great responsibilities. Come, share my joy." Then the third servant returned the one talent he had been given. The man was angry because the servant did not even try to use his talent. So the man took the talent away from him. The servant lost the gift that was given to him because he did not use it.

adapted from
Matthew
25:14–29

9

My Special Talents

God gave all of us talents, or gifts, that make us special. Circle the words below that name your special abilities. Write something else special about you in the "What else?" block. Then finish the sentences.

Swimming   Writing   Dancing   Singing

Skating   Sweeping   Praying   Reading

Smiling   Playing an instrument   Drawing   What else? *jump rop*

I like _*swimming*_ .

I am good at _*skating*_ .

Something special about me is _*my funnyness*_

I can use my talents to praise God and to help others by _*thinking*_
*of others* .

David Used His Talents

David was the greatest king in the history of Israel. He used his gifts to praise God and to help God's people. We could give him the following awards.

Best Shepherd

David took good care of his father's sheep in Bethlehem. He even killed a lion and a bear that attacked them. When Samuel was sent by God to look for a new king, young David was called in from the fields. Samuel knew that David's heart pleased God. He poured oil on David's head. This was a sign that God had chosen David.

Best Protector

David was good at using a slingshot. Once he had to fight a tall and fearsome warrior named Goliath. When David struck Goliath on the forehead with a stone, Goliath fell to the ground dead. David used his skill to protect his country. He gave glory to God.

Best Songwriter

David wrote **psalms** of praise and thanks. A psalm is a poem that was written as a song. When King Saul was sad, David used to play his music on the harp to cheer up the king.

Best King

David was crowned king after the death of King Saul. He won the love of all the people. He asked God to stay with him and rule with him. He served his country well as its leader.

We Can Help Each Other Discover Talents

Sometimes it's easy to see our talents. We might be good at sports or at showing younger children how to do things. We might be good at making other people smile or laugh.

Sometimes we don't know we have a talent until someone else says, "Hey, you're really good at that."

Developing Talents

Look at the pictures on this page. What talents does each person have? Write the talent on the line below the picture. How are they using their talents to honor God and to help and give joy to others? What could you say to each person to help them develop their talents?

training the dog

playing instrument *playing soccer*

A Moment with Jesus

Think about all the wonderful gifts that God has given you. Ask Jesus for his help in using your gifts and in seeing other people's gifts. Thank Jesus for his goodness.

Fill in the Blanks

Print the missing words in the puzzle. The sentences and the Word Bank will help you.

1. A king anointed as a boy was _____ .

2. A special ability is called a _____ .

3. God made us special because God _____ us.

4. Talents are special _____ from God.

5. We use our talents for _____ and others.

D a v i d

t a l e n t

l o v e s

g i f t s

G o d

We Remember

Why has God given you talents?
God has given me talents to praise him and to help others.

Word to Know
psalm

We Respond

I shall praise the LORD all my life.

Psalm 146:2

Building Family Faith

CHAPTER SUMMARY Each person fulfills God's plan differently. To aid us in doing his will, God gave us the necessary gifts and talents. He calls us to develop them as best we can and to use them for his praise and glory, our own good, and the good of others.

REFLECT
'Well done, my good and faithful servant. Since you were faithful in small matters, I will give you great responsibilities. Come, share your master's joy.'
Matthew 25:21

DISCUSS AS A FAMILY
• Have each family member identify the talents of the other family members.
• How can family members use their talents inside the home? outside the home?

PRAY
God, I offer you all that I am and all that I have.

DO
• Find a volunteer organization that can use your talents to help people in your community.
• Tell your children what you know about their ancestors' interests and talents.

Visit **www.ChristOurLife.org/family** for more family resources.

We Are God's Holy People

God Calls Us to Be Holy

When God our Father made us, he called us to be holy. God called us to know, love, and serve him. We serve God when we care for his creation and for all people. We are holy when we are kind and loving. We please God when we are fair and forgiving of others. Answering God's call to be holy is the way to happiness.

Long ago Jesus showed us how to know, love, and serve God our Father. Today Jesus is still with us. He is with us through the Holy Spirit and in his Church. Jesus helps us answer God's call to become his holy people. We help one another be holy and happy.

A Heart Like God's

Fill the heart with words that finish the sentence.

To be holy means to

love God
know God
serve God.

Help on the Road to Holiness

Trace the path the children are walking. Use each picture clue and the word bank to write the missing "help to holiness." Circle the happy faces in the clouds.

The _saints_ in heaven and holy people living today

The _leaders_ of the Church

prayer and the _sacraments_

The _Bible_

The Holy _Spirit_ that Jesus sent to guide the Church

WORD BANK

Bible   leaders
prayer   sacraments
saints   Spirit

Saint Francis Answered God's Call

Francis was a rich young man. He loved to have a good time. He went to parties almost every night. He wasted his time and money doing foolish things.

Then one day when he was listening to the Gospel at Mass, he saw what was really important in life. He realized that God was speaking to him. Francis believed that God was telling him to live like an apostle and preach about Jesus.

After that Francis gave away his belongings. He cared for the sick and the poor. He loved God and praised him for all the things in creation. Francis became a holy man and a much-loved saint.

Saint Francis Loved Animals

There are many stories about Saint Francis's love of animals. In one story, Francis preached to the birds. He told them to praise God for the blessings he had given them. The birds sang to show God their joy.

In another story, Francis made peace between a village and a wolf. He helped the people and the wolf see that they could be friends. He told the wolf not to hurt anyone. Then Francis asked the villagers to care for the hungry wolf. Francis showed compassion. He taught the people and the wolf to be kind to one another.

Saint Francis and Friends

Draw birds in the sky and a wolf at Francis's side.

What are some ways that you can care for animals?

Saint Clare Answered God's Call

Clare was born into a wealthy family in Assisi. She was very beautiful and gentle. The finest young men of the town wanted to marry her. But Clare had met Francis of Assisi and wanted to love God as he did. Like Francis, she was joyful and loved everything God had made.

Clare liked to be alone to think about God. She wanted to give her life to God. She gladly gave up all she had in her beautiful home. In the chapel of St. Mary of the Angels, Clare offered her life to God. Francis cut her golden hair and gave her the poor clothing of a Franciscan.

Then she was called Sister Clare and lived in a convent. She spent her whole life praying, fasting, and working for the love of God. She was brave, cheerful, and kind. She helped many people hear God's call. Other women joined her and together they formed the Poor Clares. The sisters did not own anything. They relied on the kindness of others. Clare was the leader of the community for 42 years. She inspired people to trust in God.

Once, Clare's convent and city were about to be attacked by invaders. Everyone panicked but Clare. She told people not to be afraid but to trust in Jesus.

The invaders were closing in on the community. Some were already climbing up the walls. Clare went to an open window and held up the Blessed Sacrament. At the sight of the Blessed Sacrament in Clare's hands, the invaders turned around and ran away!

A Moment with Jesus

Talk with Jesus in the quiet of your heart. Ask him to help you to be holy in everything that you say and do. Thank Jesus for showing us how to be holy.

We Answer God's Call

Saint Francis and Saint Clare answered God's call. They were holy people. They prayed and praised God. They also cared for people and for all creation. In all situations, they tried to act as Jesus would.

How might you act as Jesus would in the following situations?

3) Jennifer's mother asked her why she was late coming home from school. Jennifer had gone to Tamika's house without permission. She thought of telling her mother that she stayed after school to finish a math paper.

1) Carmen saw a group of girls huddled together on the playground, whispering and giggling. She could tell from their faces that they were talking about someone or something in a mean way. One of the girls asked Carmen to join them.

2) Jared was just about to refill his hungry cat's water and food bowls. The phone rang, and his best friend asked him to drop everything so they could go for a bike ride.

4) Max is not very good at running or catching a ball. Often he is all alone on the playground because no one wants to play with him. When Lucas got outside, he saw Max looking very lonely.

Good Questions

Ask yourself these questions to help you follow Jesus.

1. How well have I loved God?

2. How well have I loved others?

3. Did I choose not to do something that I should have done?

4. Have I done something that I know is wrong?

5. What did I do at home, at school, or in my neighborhood that kept me from acting like Jesus?

Ask the Holy Spirit to guide you in all your thoughts, words, and actions.

We Remember

What is the way to eternal happiness?
The way to eternal happiness is to know, love, and serve God.

Who shows us how to be holy?
Jesus shows us how to be holy. He helps us through the Holy Spirit and in his Church.

We Respond

God chose us in Christ to be holy and spotless in his sight.
adapted from Ephesians 1:4

Building Family Faith

CHAPTER SUMMARY God calls us to be his holy people. God gives us his Son, who is the Way, the Truth, and the Life. Jesus became man to show us how to live a holy life in both ordinary and extraordinary circumstances. Jesus sent the Holy Spirit to lead, strengthen, and form us into a holy people under the guidance of the Church.

REFLECT
"I am the way and the truth and the life. No one comes to the Father except through me."
John 14:6

DISCUSS AS A FAMILY
• What are some ways we can know what God is like?
• Name some saints. How do they help us become holy?
• Do you know anyone who is holy? Why do you think that person is holy?

PRAY
Holy Family, help our family be holy.

DO
• Take turns describing something you know about Jesus.
• Read the Bible as a family for a few minutes a day or at some special time each week.
• Ask your child to share the story of Saint Francis.
• Decide as a family to make a donation to a charity that, like Saint Francis, helps people who are poor

Visit **www.ChristOurLife.org/family** for more family resources.

CHAPTER 4

God Called Mary

Mary Helps Us Answer God's Call

Mary was a young Jewish woman. She grew up in Nazareth. She had a great love of God.

Here is a poem that tells the story of Mary's call to be God's mother.

The Annunciation

In a town called Nazareth,
Which is in Galilee,
Lived the Virgin Mary,
Joseph's bride-to-be.

Maybe she was working
And humming happily, too,
The day the angel came and said,
"Hail, the Lord is with you."

"Do not be afraid, Mary.
You are a favored one.
God has chosen you to be
The mother of his Son."

Mary said to Gabriel,
"With joy I'll do God's will."
Jesus' mother she became,
God's promise to fulfill.

God's own mother, Mary blest,
You are our mother, too.
Pray for us, your children,
And make us just like you.

Mary Says Yes to God

At the **Annunciation,** the angel Gabriel told Mary that God had chosen her to be the mother of Jesus.

Mary answered God's call with a yes. Mary said to the angel Gabriel,

> "Behold, I am the handmaid of the Lord. May it be done to me according to your word."
>
> Luke 1:38

Gabriel was a messenger sent by God.

• Who are messengers of God for you? What might they tell you?

• How can these boys and girls show that they have listened to God's messengers?

Mary will help us do God's will if we ask her. Mary is the Mother of the Church, all those who believe in her Son.

We Say Yes

Color these words. We say them to God when we do what his messengers tell us.

Mary Calls Us to Pray the Rosary

Mothers like to receive handmade gifts from their children. Sometimes children pick flowers and give them to their mothers.

Our mother Mary likes to receive a special garland, or crown of flowers, from us. This garland is the **Rosary.** Its prayers are like a garland of roses. Over and over in the Rosary, we say the beautiful words of the Annunciation to Mary: "Hail Mary, full of grace! The Lord is with you . . . "

Mary Gives a Special Message to Three Children

Lucy, Francisco, and Jacinta were shepherds who lived in Fatima, a small village in Portugal. One spring day in 1917, they were leading their sheep to a meadow when they saw a flash of lightning.

A beautiful lady appeared out of nowhere. She was dressed all in white, and her face shone like the sun. The children were amazed to see her.

The lady spoke to the children in a gentle voice. She told them, "Do not be afraid. I will do you no harm. I am of Heaven."

The lady told them to return to see her six more times. On the sixth visit she would tell them who she was and what she wanted. "Until then," she said, "recite the Rosary every day. Pray to bring peace to the world."

Lucy, Francisco, and Jacinta did as she asked. Finally, she told them, "I am the Lady of the Rosary."

Mary asked the children to tell the world to seek forgiveness for sin and to pray the Rosary. She also asked the children to tell the world to follow her example.

The Rosary Honors Jesus and Mary

People have prayed a form of the Rosary for hundreds of years. It is a wonderful prayer that many Catholics love to pray. Rosaries are **sacramentals.** A sacramental can be a word, action, or thing that brings us closer to God.

Today our Rosary has 50 Hail Marys in sets of ten (called decades). Each decade begins with an Our Father and ends with the Glory Be to the Father.

We pray the Rosary not only with words but with our minds and hearts. During each decade we think about a mystery. A mystery is an event in the life of Jesus, Mary, and the Church.

There are 20 mysteries that we think about in groups of five. The first group of mysteries are the Joyful Mysteries. The next group are the Luminous Mysteries. The third group is made up of the Sorrowful Mysteries. The last five are the Glorious Mysteries.

The Church named October the month of the Rosary. October 7 is the feast day of Our Lady of the Rosary. When we pray the Rosary, we honor Mary and come to know and love her Son Jesus better. Our faith grows stronger. We receive blessings for ourselves and for the whole world.

The Mysteries of the Rosary

Complete the crossword by naming the groups of mysteries. As you fill them in, think about why the mysteries are called Joyful, Luminous, Sorrowful, and Glorious.

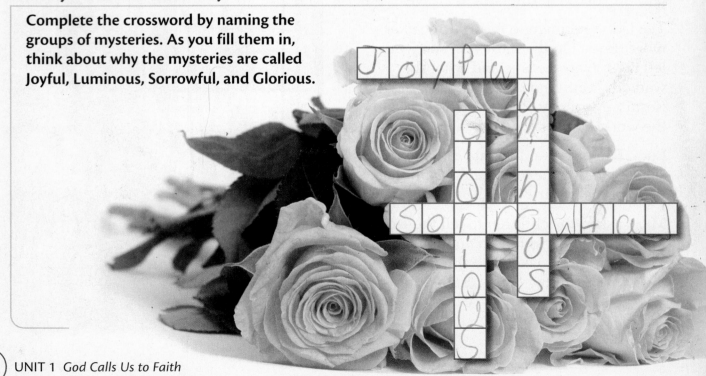

Color Your Prayers

Choose a color for both prayers and make a color key below:

Our Father

Hail Mary

Now, color in the beads of the rosary to match the prayers. What is the prayer that is prayed after the 10 Hail Marys but before Our Father?

_____

Draw in the crucifix. As you draw it, think about how much Jesus loves you.

A Decade of Love

For each bead of this decade, write the name of someone who has helped you to know and love Jesus.

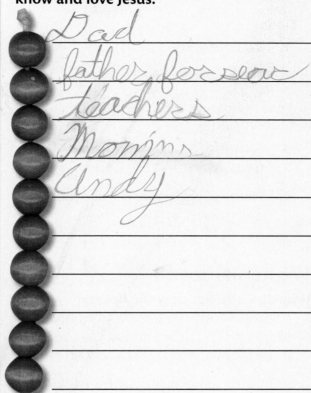

Dad

father Fosser

teachers

Momjns

Andy

A Moment with Jesus

Think about Mary's yes to God. How can you say yes to God today? Tell Jesus how happy you are that Mary is his mother and ours.

Crossword

Down

1. Jesus' Mother

2. Ten beads on which we pray the Hail Mary

Across

3. Name for an event in the life of Jesus, Mary, and the Church

4. Name of the entire set of beads and prayers

We Remember

Why do Catholics pray the Rosary?

Catholics pray the Rosary to honor Mary and to know and love her Son Jesus better.

Words to Know

Annunciation   Rosary
sacramental

We Respond

**Hail Mary, full of grace,
the Lord is with you.**

adapted from Luke 1:28

Building Family Faith

CHAPTER SUMMARY At the Annunciation Mary was asked to be the mother of Jesus, God's Son. When she said yes, she became our spiritual mother: the Mother of the Church and of all people. We show our love for Mary by responding to God's calls willingly and promptly as she did. We honor her in a special way by praying the Rosary.

REFLECT

"Behold, I am the handmaid of the Lord. May it be done to me according to your word."

Luke 1:38

DISCUSS AS A FAMILY

• What makes Mary such a good spiritual role model for us?

• How can we answer God's call to us as Mary did?

• When did God call you today, and how did you answer?

PRAY

Holy Mary, Mother of God, pray for us sinners.

DO

• Display an image or statue of Mary prominently in your home.

• Make a rosary out of beads or seeds, nuts, corn, or flowers.

• When you begin a long trip, pray the Rosary together as a family.

• At mealtimes, sing a song honoring Mary.

Visit **www.ChristOurLife.org/family** for more family resources.

Jesus Calls Us to Follow

Jesus Called the Apostles

Jesus called some men to be his special followers. This is the story as Peter, the chief apostle, might tell it:

> My brother Andrew and I are fishermen. One day as we were casting our nets into the sea, Jesus passed by. He called, "Come after me, and I will make you fishers of men." We left our nets and followed him. A little way down the shore we saw James and John, who are brothers. They were in their boats mending nets with their father. Jesus called these brothers too, and they joined us.
>
> adapted from Mark 1:16–20

Later Jesus called eight other men to be his apostles—12 in all. They came to believe that Jesus was the Son of God sent by the Father to save us. The apostles taught people the Good News. They healed the sick in Jesus' name. They became the first leaders of the Church.

Jesus Called People to Be His Disciples

Jesus also called 72 people to be his disciples. They were to help him bring all people to God our Father. Jesus looked at a field of ripe grain. He said, "The field is full of grain, but there are only a few workers. Pray that God will send workers to gather in the harvest."

adapted from Luke 10:1–2

Jesus still calls people to follow him today. He calls Christians to teach and live what he taught. He teaches us to pray that more people become Christians. Jesus wants us to pray for more priests, deacons, brothers, and sisters to serve his Church. Then he will have many helpers to spread the good news of God's love.

Jesus Called Saul to Be His Apostle

Saul did not like Christians. When he was a young man, he persecuted them cruelly. One day Saul and his friends were going to Damascus to arrest some of Jesus' followers.

On his journey, as he was nearing Damascus, a light from the sky suddenly flashed around him. He fell to the ground and heard a voice saying to him, "Saul, Saul, why are you persecuting me?" He said, "Who are you, sir?" The reply came, "I am Jesus, whom you are persecuting. Now get up and go into the city and you will be told what you must do." The men who were traveling with him stood speechless, for they heard the voice but could see no one. Saul got up from the ground, but when he opened his eyes he could see nothing; so they led him by the hand and brought him to Damascus. For three days he was unable to see, and he neither ate nor drank.

Acts of the Apostles 9:3–9

In Damascus, the Lord called out to his disciple, Ananias, to go to Saul who had been taken to the house of Judas. Ananias was afraid because he knew that Saul had done terrible things. But the Lord told Ananias that he had chosen Saul to teach many people about him. So Ananias obeyed and went to Saul. He laid his hands on Saul and said:

> "Saul, my brother, the Lord has sent me, Jesus who appeared to you on the way by which you came, that you may regain your sight and be filled with the holy Spirit."

Acts of the Apostles 9:17

Immediately Saul was able to see again! Ananias baptized Saul. Saul began to preach in all the **synagogues** saying, "Jesus is the Son of God." Saul was very different now. He became known as Paul.

The Road to Damascus

Draw a line tracing Saul's journey from Jerusalem to Damascus.

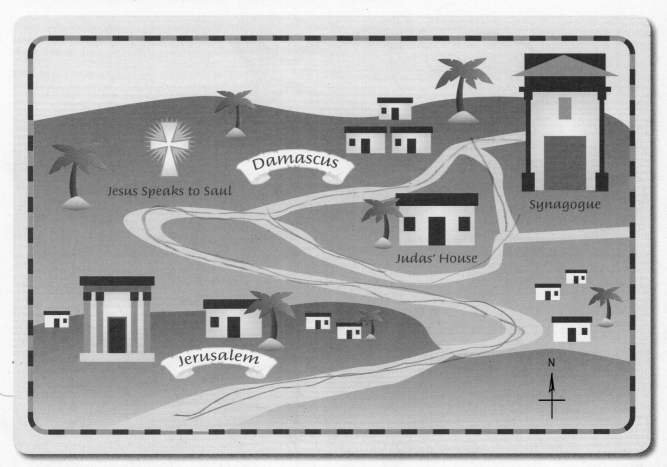

We Remember

What is an apostle?
An apostle is one of the people specially chosen by Jesus to spread his message.

What is a disciple?
A disiciple is a follower of Jesus.

What does Jesus call Christians to help him do?
Jesus calls Christians to help him spread the good news of God's love.

Word to Know
synagogue

We Respond

Here I am, Lord. I come to do your will.

adapted from Psalm 40:8–9

Go Fishing

For each of the fish below, write something that you can do to share God's love with the world.

pray

love

help

get sacrament

give joy

go to church

be cined not selfish

A Secret Message from God

Find 34 squares this size: ☐ Color them black to see God's message.

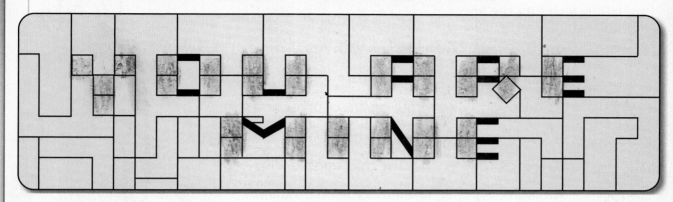

God Calls Us to Be His

Fill the clouds with names of people called by God. To climb the mountain, put in words that tell how we respond to God's call. Use the Word Bank.

WORD BANK

Abraham	love	apostles	Mary
David	Paul	know	Ruth
Peter	Francis	disciples	serve
Gabriel	Clare	us	care

A B R A H A M ,
D I S C I P L E S

D A V I D   F R A N C I S

P A U L   G A B R I E L   D

U S   C L A R E   K N O W

M A R Y   L O V E

R U T H   P

A P O S T L E S   S E R V E

P E T E R   C A R E

R

Find the Pairs

Match the person on the left with the description on the right. Write the matching letter on the line.

_e_	**1.** Clare	**a.**	had a son with Abraham
_b_	**2.** Abraham	**b.**	loved animals
_h_	**3.** Ruth	**c.**	wrote psalms of praise and thanks
_f_	**4.** David	**d.**	is the Mother of God
_f_	**5.** Francis	**e.**	was the chief apostle
_a_	**6.** Sarah	**f.**	saved a city from invaders
_d_	**7.** Mary	**g.**	went with Naomi to Bethlehem
_c_	**8.** Peter	**h.**	was baptized by Ananias
_g_	**9.** Paul	**i.**	was told that God would make of him a great nation

Word Search

Find and circle 13 words that tell what Jesus' disciples do. The words go across and down.

```
L T R U S T P B S S
I C H E A U R T T A
S O T E A C A R E C
T B S T U D Y A A R
E E H E L P L S L I
N Y A T H A N K O F
F O R G I V E W V I
A R E P R A I S E C
L I E C H E A T R E
```

We are God's Holy People

Leader: Let us begin our prayer with the Sign of the Cross.

All: In the name of the Father, and of the Son, and of the Holy Spirit.

Amen.

Reader 1: God called Abraham to believe that Abraham's family would be God's people. God called Ruth to faith. God called David to serve him and his chosen people. God called Mary, a woman of faith, to be the Mother of the Savior.

Reader 2: Jesus called Peter and the other apostles to lead his people. He called disciples to carry on his work. He called Paul to bring others to the faith. He called Saint Francis and Saint Clare. God calls us at Baptism. We belong to the people of faith. We are Catholics who follow Jesus.

Reader 3: A reading from Paul's Letter to the Ephesians.

. . . you are fellow citizens with the holy ones and members of the household of God, built upon the foundation of the apostles and prophets, with Christ Jesus himself as the capstone. Through him the whole structure is held together and grows into a temple sacred in the Lord.

(Ephesians 2:19–21)

The Word of the Lord.

All: Thanks be to God.

Leader: Let us build a structure to show how we form the Church with all the holy people of God. As you place your card, read the names on it and say, ". . . belong to God's holy people."

Side 1: God, we believe in you. We trust you.

Side 2: Jesus, we follow you. Deepen our love.

Side 1: Holy Spirit, strengthen our faith.

Side 2: Mary, Mother of the Church, pray for us.

Leader: Let us listen to God and pray in our hearts.

(Silent Reflection)

Leader: Let us bless the Lord.

All: Thanks be to God.

(Song)

Family Feature

Mary the Parent

There are two things we should always remember about Mary.  First, think of how intimately she lived with God, whom she carried in her womb. She continues to live in intimate love with her son in heaven. No one knows Jesus better than his mother.

We should also remember that Mary was and is a parent. Mary gave birth to Jesus, fed him, dressed him, raised him, walked and talked with him. She did what all parents do, and she did it very well. In this Family Feature, we will talk about how we as parents can learn from Mary, the parent.

MARIAN FEASTS

January 1
Solemnity of Mary, Mother of God

March 25
Annunciation

May 31
Visitation

**Saturday after the
Second Sunday after Pentecost**
Immaculate Heart of Mary

July 16
Our Lady of Mount Carmel

August 15
Assumption

August 22
Queenship of the Virgin Mary

September 8
Birth of Mary

October 7
Our Lady of the Rosary

November 21
Presentation of Mary

December 8
Immaculate Conception

December 12
Our Lady of Guadalupe

Family Feature

The Annunciation

God chose Mary, but we should also remember that Mary made a choice as well. Mary chose to become Jesus'  mother. Luke 1:26–38 tells the story of how an angel appeared to her in the tiny village of Nazareth and told her that she was to conceive a child by the power of the Holy Spirit and her

The Annunciatinon, Jamestown ND

child would be "Son of the Most High." Could there be a greater call to service? She surely knew that this possible future involved pain and suffering as well as love and joy. But she courageously embraced God's plan, saying, "I am the handmaid of the Lord. May it be done to me according to your word."

Parenthood means continually saying yes to challenges. When we bring children into the world, we say yes to great responsibilities without knowing exactly what they will entail or how we will face them. We certainly have our doubts sometimes about our ability to fulfill them. Mary shows us how to say yes with faith and courage.

The Birth of Jesus

The story of Jesus' birth is told in Luke 2: 1–20, with additional details in Matthew 2. The circumstances surrounding Jesus' birth could hardly have been more difficult: an arduous journey, a birth in a makeshift setting far from home, and a sudden flight into exile to escape a murderous Herod. Yet despite the tumult and trouble, Mary and Joseph welcomed the baby Jesus into their lives with joy.

Our lives are forever changed by the birth of our children. In some ways, we trade our old lives for new ones. This is joyous, but it can also be bittersweet to  turn our backs on a life we might have had and welcome new life and a new family. That is why generous welcoming is the essential virtue of parents.

Finding Jesus in the Temple

In Luke 2: 41–52, we learn how Mary faced every parent's nightmare—a lost child. On a family trip to Jerusalem, the twelve-year-old Jesus was missing in the turbulent city. After three days of frantic searching, Mary and Joseph found him in conversation with teachers in the Temple. Jesus calmly greets his anxious parents with a pointed question, "Did you not know that I must be in my Father's house?"

Jesus had his own destiny, independent of Mary and Joseph's. Mary understood that Jesus was not just her child. He belonged to God. It is always hard to decide when to protect a child and when to let the child be independent. We can ask Mary for help finding the grace to make these choices wisely.

The Miracle at Cana

As a grown man, Jesus began his public ministry by changing water into wine at a wedding feast. However, as we can see in John 2:1–12, he probably wouldn't have performed this miracle without the prodding of his mother. Jesus resisted his mother's urging, saying, "My hour has not yet come." On that night, Mary seemed to understand his mission better than he did, so she gave him a nudge. She insisted and Jesus worked the miracle. She was still his mother, after all.

We will always be our children's parents, even when they are adults. We will be there to share our experience and knowledge, to guide them on the difficult paths we have walked before them, and sometimes we will give them a push in the right direction when they need it. We can look to Mary as the example of how to do this.

Visit **www.ChristOurLife.org/family** for more family resources.

Family Feature

Help Mary and Joseph Find Jesus in Jerusalem

Mary and Joseph are looking for Jesus. Help them by guiding them to the Temple where Jesus is speaking with the teachers. Guide them by drawing a line to Jesus.

God Is Great and Good

For the LORD is the great God, the great king over all gods,

Whose hand holds the depths of the earth;

  who owns the tops of the mountains.

The sea and dry land belong to God, who made them,

  formed them by hand.

Psalm 95:3–5

A Letter Home

Dear Parents and Family,

Getting to know God is a lifelong adventure. So much about him is revealed in Scripture, in our Catholic tradition, and in the life stories of saints. In Unit 2, the children will study the basic truths of our faith in the Apostles' Creed. They will learn some of the characteristics of God, then discuss how to respond to him with love and respect.

The children will meet God as Creator, and they are encouraged to trust his will. They will hear Old Testament accounts of God's relationship with his people whom he created and the saving deeds he performed for them. The lessons establish the connection between God as visible in creation, then as perfectly revealed in the teachings and saving deeds of Jesus, which are articulated in the New Testament.

In Chapter 6, "We Believe in God," the children will learn the Apostles' Creed and the central mysteries of our faith. You might add the Apostles' Creed to your own family prayers. You can find it on the inside front cover of your child's book. You can also find it under Catholic Tradition within the Resources section at www.ChristOurLife.org.

Trust in God is encouraged in the story of his promise to Moses and the Israelites. The children learn the wisdom of relying on God, who is both powerful and loving. They also come to know God as holy, great, all-knowing, and all-present. They will grow in reverence for him and his name as they review the Second Commandment. (You shall not take the name of the Lord your God in vain.)

The unit concludes with an examination of justice and mercy, both characteristics of God's everlasting love for us. The children will learn that God shares with us today the same justice and mercy that he granted the Israelites so long ago. They will also discover examples from Jesus and the saints. If you use the words *justice* and *mercy* to identify these concepts when they are lived out in your family, you will help make them real for your child.

At the end of each chapter in this unit, the children will bring home a review of the chapter along with the Building Family Faith feature. This feature gives you a quick review of what your child has learned and offers practical ways to reinforce the lesson at home so that the whole family may benefit. At the end of the unit, the children will bring home the Family Feature handout to help nurture the family's faith at home.

Visit **www.ChristOurLife.org/family** for more family resources.

We Believe in God

Apostles' Creed

I believe in God, the Father
almighty,
creator of heaven and earth.
I believe in Jesus Christ, his only
Son, our Lord.
He was conceived by the power of
the Holy Spirit
and born of the Virgin Mary
He suffered under Pontius Pilate,
was crucified, died, and was buried.
He descended to the dead.
On the third day he rose again.
He ascended into heaven,
and is seated at the right hand
of the Father.
He will come again to judge the
living and the dead.
I believe in the Holy Spirit,
the holy catholic Church,
the communion of saints,
the forgiveness of sins,
the resurrection of the body,
and the life everlasting.

Amen.

We Profess Our Faith in the Creed

At each Sunday Eucharist the priest invites us to profess, or declare, our faith. We, as people of God, stand and pray the Creed.

The form of the Creed that we pray at Mass is called the Nicene Creed. Another form is the **Apostles' Creed**.

A **creed** tells what we believe as Catholics. By praying the Creed, we profess our belief in the great mysteries of our faith.

Mysteries of Our Faith

A **mystery** is a religious truth we cannot completely understand with our minds. With God's help we can begin to understand it with our hearts.

Everything that we believe, say, and do as Catholics comes from these great mysteries.

Complete the missing words to tell the main truths God has revealed.

1. God is the F A t h e r , who created all things.

2. God is the S o n , who redeemed us by his death and Resurrection.

3. God is the Holy S p i r i t , who makes us holy.

4. The C r e e d s was founded by Jesus to teach us and to make us holy.

God Is Three Persons in One

One of the great mysteries of our faith is that there are three Persons in God. We call this the mystery of the Trinity. God is Father, Son, and Holy Spirit. All three Persons are great, good, and loving. We praise and thank the one God in our prayer.

A Moment with Jesus

Read the Scripture passage quietly.

> As high as the heavens are above the earth,
> so high are my ways above your ways
> and my thoughts above your thoughts.
>
> Isaiah 55:9

Thank Jesus for helping us know God's mysteries better.

God Our Creator Is Good

We believe God made all of creation. God made the universe and the planets and the stars. He made all the creatures, plants, and rocks on earth. His most special creation was the human family. God made us in his own image. He made us because he loves each one of us.

When God made the universe, he was happy with all his creation. So everything we see tells us something about him.

Look at the pictures of God's creation. What can you learn about God from each one? Write a word below each picture that says how it makes you feel about God.

loving   beautiful

peaceful   earth   sweet

God Kept His Promises to the Israelites

To Abraham, the father of the Chosen People, God had promised,

> "I will give this land of Canaan to your children."
>
> adapted from Genesis 12:7

After many years the children of Abraham moved to Egypt. The Bible refers to the children of Abraham as the **Hebrews** and later as the **Israelites.** Pharaoh, the king of Egypt, became afraid of them. He thought they might become too powerful, so he made them slaves.

The Israelites were slaves in Egypt for many years. Then God chose Moses to lead them to freedom.

The story the Jewish people tell about their escape is in the Bible. In this story God spoke to Moses from a flaming bush. God said,

> "I have seen how my people suffer in Egypt. Now I have come to free them. I will bring them into a good land, the land of Canaan. You must lead my people out of Egypt. Tell Pharaoh what I have said."
>
> adapted from Exodus 3:7–10

Moses told Pharaoh God's message, but Pharaoh wouldn't let the Israelites go. Instead he made them work even harder. Moses warned Pharaoh that terrible things would happen, but Pharaoh still refused to free his slaves.

God sent many signs of his power. Even then, Pharaoh wouldn't let God's people go. Finally, God told Moses to prepare his people for one more sign. Each family should kill a lamb and put its blood on the door of the house. God said,

> "It is the Passover of the LORD! This night every first-born son will die. But the blood will mark the houses where you are. Death will pass over you."
>
> adapted from Exodus 12:11–13

That night every oldest son died—even Pharaoh's son—but the Israelites were passed over. Then Pharaoh and all the Egyptians begged them to leave. God helped Moses lead his people across the Red Sea through the desert to Canaan.

God is good and faithful to all of us. He made promises to us that he will keep, just as he kept his promise to the Israelites.

God Keeps His Promise to Us

God promised to send us a Savior. God kept this promise. He sent his Son to save us from sin. His name, *Jesus*, means "God saves." Jesus' suffering, death, and Resurrection freed us from sin. He won eternal life for us. That means that we can live forever with God.

Now we are God's people, on a journey to be with him forever. Jesus shows us the way through the Holy Spirit. He helps us overcome temptations. Jesus has a place ready for us in heaven.

Our journey is like that of the Israelites. As God kept his promise to them, he will keep his promise to us. God will lead us to eternal life if we trust in his promise and do what he tells us.

We Can Grow in Faith

Complete these sentences about ways we grow in faith. Use the words in the Word Bank.

WORD BANK

profess
help
obey
Bible

Holy Communion
pray
Church

1. We read God's Word in the ___Bible___.

2. We receive ___Holy Communion___ at Mass.

3. We listen when the ___church___ ___preast___ teaches us.

4. We tell what we believe as Christians, or ___profess___ our faith.

5. We exercise our faith when we ___obey___ God.

6. We live our faith when we ___help___ others.

7. We speak to God and listen to God when we ___pray___.

Studying your faith helps it grow. This book will help you learn what Catholics believe.

These children are living their faith by participating in a religious procession.

Stand Up for Your Beliefs

We are called to profess our faith by what we say and do. Sometimes this takes courage. What are some times when we need courage to profess our faith? Who are people that showed courage by living their faith?

Checking Your Understanding

Put the words in order to form sentences about God. Write the sentences on the lines.

1. _One God almighty created everything_.

        created   One   everything   God   almighty

2. _There are three persons in one God_.

        Persons   God   three   There   are   in   one

3. _God keeps all his promises_.

        promises   keeps   God   his   all

4. _God wants us to obey and trust him_.

        God   us   trust   wants   to   him   obey   and

We Remember

Where are the main truths of our faith found?

The main truths of our faith are found in the Creed.

What does God promise us?

God promises that those who believe in him and obey him will live with him forever in heaven.

Words to Know
Apostles' Creed
creed
Hebrews
Israelites
mystery

We Respond

Jesus, I hope in you.

Building Family Faith

CHAPTER SUMMARY The chief truths of the Catholic faith are found in the Creed. One of the most important of these truths is that God is faithful to us. He keeps his promises.

REFLECT
Jesus told her, "I am the resurrection and the life; whoever believes in me, even if he dies, will live, and everyone who lives and believes in me will never die. Do you believe this?"

John 11:25–26

DISCUSS AS A FAMILY
- Choose one of the statements of belief in the Apostles' Creed (page 37). Discuss what it means.
- Talk about a time when someone kept a promise they had made to you. How did you feel when the promise was kept? What did you say to the person?

- What is the right response to a God who keeps his promises?

PRAY
"The promises of the LORD I will sing forever,"

Psalm 89:2

DO
Pray the Apostles' Creed together.

Visit **www.ChristOurLife.org/family** for more family resources.

God Is Powerful and Loving

The Bible has many stories about how God shows his power and love. This story is about Moses and the Israelites at the Red Sea.

God Saves the Israelites with His Power

Pharaoh changed his mind about letting the Israelite people go. He sent his army to bring them back.

The Israelites were afraid when they saw Pharaoh's army. "Do not be afraid," Moses told them. "The Lord will win a great victory for you today." God said to Moses, "Stretch out your hand over the sea and split it so that the people may pass through it."

Moses did what God told him. All night God sent a strong wind. He made a path of dry land. The Israelites marched into the sea with the water like walls on both sides of them.

All of Pharaoh's horses and soldiers went into the sea after the Israelites. God said to Moses, "Stretch out your hand over the sea again." Moses did, and the sea flowed back upon Pharaoh's army.

The Israelites rejoiced. Their all-powerful God had saved them.

based on Exodus 14:10–28

Moses and the men sang a song of victory and praise to God while the women danced.

Moses' Song of Victory

I will sing to the LORD, for he has won a
    great victory!
The horses and their riders he has cast
    into the sea.
The LORD gives me strength and courage,
    and he has been my Savior.
Who is like you, O LORD?
Who is like you, worker of wonders?
In your mercy you led the people you saved;
    in your strength you guided them to
    their own land.
             adapted from Exodus 15:1–2,11,13

We Trust God's Power

Just like Moses and the Israelites, we also trust in God's power. God is all-powerful and frees us from our greatest enemy, sin. God helps us win battles against it. He keeps us safe on our journey to him.

Fill in the missing words.
You can find them on the pyramid.

God is all _powerful_.

God helps those who _trust_

and _obey_ him.

I will ask God to _help_ me.

help
powerful
trust
obey

God Fed the Israelites

After the Israelites escaped Pharaoh's army, they had to travel a long way through the desert. They felt tired, hungry, and thirsty. God said, "I will rain down bread from heaven."

The next morning something that looked like frost covered the ground. "What is this?" the Israelites asked. Moses told them, "This is the bread the Lord has given you to eat."

Each morning this white bread covered the ground. The Israelites called it manna. The Lord told them, "Take only what you need for one day." He wanted his people to trust in his care. They showed their trust by doing what God told them.

God fed his people manna until they came to Canaan. He looked after them like a loving father and a caring mother.

based on Exodus 16:1–35

God Feeds Us

God shows loving care for us today. He feeds us with the Body and Blood of his own Son, Jesus, in the Holy Eucharist. Jesus is the bread from heaven. Once he said,

> "I am the living bread that came down from heaven; whoever eats this bread will live forever; and the bread that I will give is my flesh for the life of the world."
>
> John 6:51

This heavenly food nourishes the life we received in Baptism. It strengthens us on our journey through this world to the promised land of heaven.

In Holy Communion we are united with Jesus. He shares himself with us in love. He makes us more like himself. He also comes to make us more united as his people. God feeds us so that we can serve the needs of others.

God Makes a Covenant of Love

God made a **covenant** with the Israelites. He would be their God, and they would be his people. The Bible tells us about this important agreement.

The Israelites came to Mt. Sinai in the desert and set up camp. Then Moses climbed the mountain to God. God gave him this message for the people:

> "You have seen how I saved you. If you listen to my words, you shall be dearer to me than all other people. You will be a holy nation."

On the third day God gave the people the commandments. They answered,

> "Everything the LORD has said, we will do."

Later God gave Moses the law written on stone tablets. The people loved God's law. They knew it would guide them to happiness. It showed God's love for them.

The Israelites were joined to God as his own people. He was their God, and they belonged to him. They would worship him and obey his laws. God would bless them and care for them. God and his people were united in a covenant of love.

based on Exodus 19:1–20:17; 24:1–12

We Have a Covenant with God

We are the people of God today. We too are joined to God in a covenant of love. Through Baptism, God has made us his own children. We have received a share in his life. We have promised to live by his laws and to follow Jesus. God has promised that we will live with him forever in heaven.

Keeping the Covenant

How are these children keeping their covenant of love? What are some things that you can do?

An Acrostic on Covenant

Write the words where they belong in the puzzle.

God c __e l l s__ us to have faith in him.

God showed his __p__ o __w e r__ in saving his people.

God made a covenant of __l o__ v __e__ with us.

We are God's holy __p__ e __o p l e__ .

God makes us his __o w__ n people.

The commandments are God's __l__ a __w s__ .

Our agreement with God is a __c o v e__ n __a n t__ of love.

We became God's children at our __b a p__ t __i s m__ .

A Moment with Jesus

What is one thing that you can do today to show that you are thankful?

Complete the Sentences

Write the letter of the word that correctly completes the sentence.

a. Jesus   b. Moses
c. Israelites   d. Pharaoh

___b___ led the people to the promised land.

___d___ sent an army after the Israelites.

___a___ said "I am the living bread."

Moses and the ___c___ received manna from heaven.

We Remember

What is our covenant of love with God?
Our covenant of love is our agreement with God. God makes us his children, and we obey his laws and follow Jesus.

What are the commandments?
The commandments are God's laws of love.

Words to Know
covenant   worship

We Respond

I will celebrate your promises forever, Lord.
I will always proclaim your love.

adapted from Psalm 89:2

Building Family Faith

CHAPTER SUMMARY God saved his people from oppression, fed them when they were hungry, and made a covenant of love with them. We recall these deeds when we celebrate the Sacrament of the Eucharist.

REFLECT
In your mercy you led the people you redeemed; in your strength you guided them to your holy dwelling.

Exodus 15:13

DISCUSS AS A FAMILY
• We have many agreements with friends, teachers, adults. Which are the hardest ones to keep? Which are the easiest?
• What is God's part of the covenant we have with him? What is our part?
• How is our covenant with God like the agreements we make with each other in our family?

PRAY
Praise the LORD, who is so good;
    God's love endures forever.
Psalm 136:1

DO
Make a written agreement, or covenant, with a family member to exchange services or favors this coming week. Each evening check on how each person has kept his or her part of the bargain.

Visit **www.ChristOurLife.org/family** for more family resources.

God Is Holy and Great

The Lord Our God Is Holy

Have you ever felt God's holy presence in a special way? It fills us with wonder and awe.

How did God first speak to Moses? God said from the burning bush: "Come no nearer! Remove the sandals from your feet, for the place where you stand is holy ground. I am the God of your fathers." Moses hid his face, for he was afraid.

adapted from Exodus 3:5–6

Before the all-holy God we feel small and helpless, like Moses. We fear God, and it is natural that we should. But our fear of God is full of *love* and *praise*. We know that the great and holy God loves us.

God revealed, or showed, his holiness through his Son, Jesus. Jesus is the holy one of God.

> **Unscramble the words to find out how Jesus' holiness is known.**
>
> 1. Jesus performed CREAMSIL.
>
> _____
>
> 2. Jesus did works of SNOIHLES.
>
> _____
>
> 3. Jesus SERO from the ADDE.
>
> _____

God's Holy Name

God revealed his holy name to Moses. Moses said to the Lord, "When the Israelites ask your name, what am I to tell them?"

The Lord answered,

> ## "I am who am."
>
> Exodus 3:14

Respecting God's Name

The Second Commandment tells us to speak God's name with love and respect. It tells us to honor everything related to God. We worship God with love and praise because he is the holy one.

We show our belief in God when we call upon his name. An example is when we pray the Sign of the Cross.

Write the three names of God that we pray in the Sign of the Cross.

In the name of the
___father___ ,

and of the
___son___ ,

and of the
___holy Spirit___ .

Amen.

The people called God **Yahweh** because that is the Hebrew word meaning "I am who am."

Names were very important to the Israelites. A person's name told not only who he or she was. It revealed something about the person. God's name tells who he is. He is God, the holy one. God's name means God himself.

A Special Home

The great God was with his chosen people. He told Moses, "My people must build me a special home. I wish to live among them."

When the home, or dwelling, was complete, God gave a special sign of his presence. A bright cloud came to rest over the dwelling that they had built.

It was by this cloud that God led his people on their journey. When the cloud rose, the Israelites took down their tents and the dwelling. They followed the cloud until it stopped. Then they pitched their tents and put the dwelling in the center of the camp.

Jesus Makes His Home Among Us

Later, God came to live among his people in an even more wonderful way.

God's own Son was born on earth and became man. Jesus was God living among his people. He shared their work, play, joys, and sadness. God was still caring for his people.

Jesus still dwells among his people. He is with us in his Church through the Holy Spirit. He is with us in a special way when we celebrate Mass and receive Holy Communion. Jesus also dwells in our hearts by grace. He is with us, guiding us and caring for us with his power and his love.

God Is Everywhere

God is so great! Besides being in special places, God is also everywhere. This is wonderful because God is with all creation and with every one of the people he has created and loves.

God Knows All Things About His People

God knows all things. He knows everything about each person. God knows what we think and how we feel. He knows even the secrets of our hearts. He knows when we are in need of help even when we don't tell anyone. God is with us and wants to help us.

God Knows All About the Universe

God, who created the universe, knows all about it and loves it very much. He knows how mountains came to be and how seeds grow. He knows the center of the earth and the most distant star.

God knows everything that is happening now. He knows about things that happened long ago. He knows all that will happen in the future. And God uses everything for our good.

Psalm Prayer

Where can I run from you, O God?
Where can I hide from your presence?

If I could fly to the highest heavens,
You would be there.

If I could sink down into the heart of the earth,
You would be present there.

If I were to sail to the ends of the sea,
Your hand would still be guiding me.

Not even darkness can hide me from you.
For you there is no darkness at all.

O Lᴏʀᴅ, you know everything about me.
You know when I sit and when I stand.

You see all that I am thinking.
You know all my ways.

Even before a word comes from my mouth,
You know all about it.

You are behind me and before me and all around me.
You rest your hand upon me.

Your knowledge is so wonderful, O God!
It is too great for me to understand.

adapted from Psalm 139:1–12

A Moment with Jesus

Read the Psalm Prayer quietly. What is
one place that you are glad that Jesus is
there with you?

We Give God First Place in Our Lives

God is both holy and great. We show our belief in God by putting him first in whatever we do or say. There are many people—religious sisters and brothers, lay people, and priests—to whom we can look as role models. Saint Elizabeth Ann Seton is one example of a dedicated Christian leader.

Saint Elizabeth Ann Seton

Saint Elizabeth Ann Seton was born in 1774. Her parents taught her to love and to serve people who were poor. They taught her the importance of prayer and reading the Bible. They taught her how to put God first in her life.

Elizabeth faced many difficulties in her life. Even though life was hard, she still put God first. She raised five children by herself. She started a school. Later she started a religious community, the Sisters of Charity of Saint Joseph. They helped people in schools, hospitals, orphanages, and anywhere else God called them to serve.

> "Live simply, so that all may simply live."
>
> Saint Elizabeth Ann Seton

Help Along the Way

Write some things that can help you when you face difficult decisions.

dance for joy

sing

jump

Can You Find Signs of the Holy?

Unscramble the words to find persons and things used in the service of God.
(*Clue:* **Look at the pictures.**)

1. streip _____

2. taral _____

3. celaich _____

4. cixfuric _cruifex_____

5. Bleib _Bible_____

6. tancor _cantor_____

Write down three other people or things that remind you of God's holiness.

_dog_____
_Mom_____
_Dad_____

Praise to you, O holy God!

You are present everywhere.

You know all things.

You are so great.

How Well Do You Remember?

Complete these sentences with the correct words. One letter belongs in each box.

1. God is h o l y.

2. God is present e v r e y w h e r e.

3. God knows a l l things.

4. God is a l w a s y with us.

5. God knows even the secrets of our h e a r t s.

6. God is present in a special way in c h u r c h.

We Remember

What is God like?
God is holy and great. He is everywhere and always near. He knows all things.

How does the Second Commandment tell us to show respect for God?
The Second Commandment tells us to show respect for God by honoring his holy name. It tells us to respect everything related to God.

Word to Know
Yahweh

We Respond

Praise the LORD: the LORD is good!
Sing to God's name; it is gracious!

Psalm 135:3

Building Family Faith

CHAPTER SUMMARY God is all-holy and all-powerful. He knows all things. Yet this mighty and holy God loves us with a Father's love. He is present in our world, in our family, and in each of our hearts.

REFLECT

LORD, you have probed me, you know me:
you know when I sit and stand;
you understand my thoughts from afar.
Psalm 139: 1–2

DISCUSS AS A FAMILY

- When do we feel closest to God?
- Ask each family member to pick a favorite prayer. Talk about why he or she picked it.
- When have we felt the power and majesty of God?

PRAY

Holy God, you are our loving Father. Make us holy, as you are holy.

DO

Visit a church when it is quiet. Open yourselves to the peace and grandeur of God.

Visit **www.ChristOurLife.org/family** for more family resources.

God Is Just and Merciful

Our Just and Merciful God Loves Us

Our just God gave the people the covenant and blessed them with peace and happiness. When the people kept the covenant, they lived in peace with God and each other. But when the Israelites did not keep the covenant, their sins brought trouble.

Their rulers became selfish and foolish. The people were no longer united, and the nation became weak. Enemies attacked. The people suffered for their actions. They needed God's help to return to the covenant.

God is both just and merciful. He knew that his people were weak when it came to resisting sin. He was always ready to forgive them and to take them back.

Moses often spoke to God on behalf of his people. He prayed, "Lord, have mercy on your people. Do not look upon their sins."

The people cried to God for mercy too. God always had pity on them. He forgave them again and again.

Psalm Prayer

Bless the LORD, O my soul,
    and remember all his kindness.
The LORD is merciful and kind,
    slow to anger and most loving.
God does not punish us
    as our sins and wrongs deserve.
Just as the heavens are high above the earth
    so great is his kindness toward
        those who fear him.
God puts our sins farther away
    than the east is from the west.
As a father has pity on his children,
    so the LORD has pity
        on those who fear him.
        adapted from Psalm 103:2,8–13

Jesus Is the Good Shepherd

Jesus told his disciples that they must be like a good shepherd. A shepherd must protect and care for the sheep in his flock.

What kinds of things do shepherds do to care for their sheep? What does a good shepherd do if a sheep gets lost?

In the Bible, Jesus says that he is the Good Shepherd and we are his sheep. He cares for us and watches out for us. When we keep his laws of love, he blesses us with peace. Sometimes we get lost because we sin. Jesus forgives our sins and calls us to be sorry. As the Good Shepherd, he welcomes us back and cares for us.

Jesus Revealed the Father's Justice and Mercy

Jesus did many things to show the **justice** and mercy of God our Father. He showed justice when he was angry at those who dishonored the Temple, his Father's house. He showed mercy when he healed the sick and forgave sinners.

To show that God is *just*, Jesus told a story about a rich man and a poor man. The rich man had fine clothes and plenty of good food. The poor man, called Lazarus, longed to have the leftovers from the rich man's table. The rich man would not give him any. Then one day Lazarus died and went to a place of happiness. When the rich man died, he went to a place of suffering. The rich man suffered for not sharing his wealth on earth. Lazarus was rewarded with happiness.

Jesus tells us of God's *mercy* in many stories. Once, Jesus said, there was a woman who had 10 coins, but then lost one. She carefully searched her house. When she found the lost coin, she celebrated with her friends. Jesus wanted to teach us that God our Father is like the woman who lost the coin. When we are lost, God carefully searches for us. He is merciful and calls us to be sorry for our sins. When we are sorry, we celebrate God's forgiveness in the Sacrament of Penance and Reconciliation.

Break the Code

Using the code below, complete the sentence.

C	E	F	I	J	L	M	R	S	T	U
1	2	3	4	5	6	7	8	9	10	11

We believe that our God is

__ __ __ __ __ __ __ __
7 2 8 1 4 3 11 6

and __ __ __ __
    5 11 9 10

Just like Jesus

Jesus wants us to be as just and merciful as he is. We are just when we treat others as God treats us. He is always caring for us and loving us. We are merciful when we forgive others as our heavenly Father forgives us. We show his merciful love when we help those in need.

Saint Vincent de Paul

Vincent de Paul showed Jesus' mercy by caring for people who were sick or in prison. He organized a group of people to collect and distribute food and money to people who had little. Vincent believed that it was a matter of justice for people who had all they needed to help those who were in need.

Saint Louise de Marillac

Louise de Marillac worked with Vincent de Paul. Together they started the Daughters of Charity. This community of sisters helped Vincent in all his works of mercy. They worked in homes, hospitals, and wherever else there was a need. The Daughters of Charity are still helping people today.

A Challenge for You!

Complete this puzzle about our just and merciful God. Use the clues.

1. When we forgive others, we show _____ .

2. Jesus told us to _____ one another.

3. God calls us to be _____ for our sins.

4. When we obey God's commandments, God gives us _____ .

5. We learn about the Good Shepherd in the _____ .

6. When the Israelites were sorry they sinned, God _____ them.

7. We are _____ when we treat each other fairly.

8. Jesus treated the poor man named _____ with justice.

M
E
R
C
I
F
U
L

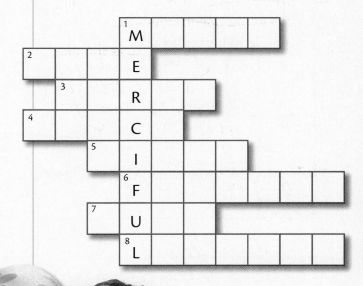

We Remember

How is God just?

God shows his justice by giving us the covenant that shows us how we can live in peace with him and one another.

How is God merciful?

God shows us his mercy by forgiving our sins and calling us to be sorry.

Word to Know
justice

We Respond

I will treat others in the same way God treats me: loving me and caring for me. I will forgive others as my heavenly Father forgives me and will help those in need.

Word Search

Circle 12 words in the puzzle that describe God.

```
T  R  E  M  F  P  O  W  E  R  F  U  L
A  G  R  E  A  T  R  U  T  H  F  U  L
M  E  R  C  I  F  U  L  L  A  P  I  M
L  J  U  S  T  G  D  T  O  R  P  E  C
R  O  S  W  H  O  L  Y  V  T  V  W  I
U  T  M  I  F  O  R  G  I  V  I  N  G
S  B  D  S  U  D  Z  P  N  R  E  T  O
C  O  R  E  L  J  M  I  G  H  T  Y  N
```

Then write the three words that you like best.

holy

powerful

merciful

What Is God Like?

In the box below are some of the wonderful truths about God. Next to it are passages from the Bible. Write the phrase from the box that matches what each passage tells us about God.

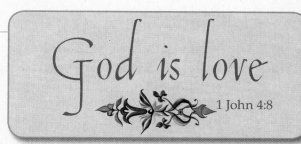

God is love

1 John 4:8

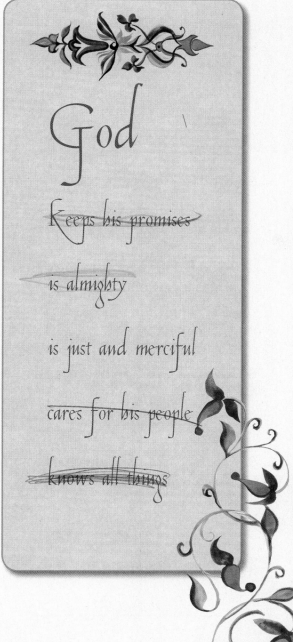

God

Keeps his promises

is almighty

is just and merciful

cares for his people

knows all things

1. "I will save you with my mighty acts." (adapted from Exodus 6:6)

   God *is almighty* .

2. "I will give you the land of Canaan as I promised your father, Abraham." (adapted from Exodus 6:8)

   God *keeps his promises* .

3. "Pharaoh would not listen just as the LORD had foretold." (adapted from Exodus 7:13)

   God *knows all things* .

4. "This is the bread which the LORD has given you to eat." (Exodus 16:15)

   God *cares for all people* .

5. "The LORD is a merciful God, slow to anger and rich in kindness, forgiving sin." (adapted from Exodus 34:6–7)

   God *is just and merciful* .

Make a Journey

Fill in the blanks with the words in the sun.
Find your score. Circle the place you reached.

10	Promised Land
8 or 9	Mount Sinai
6 or 7	Desert
4 or 5	Red Sea

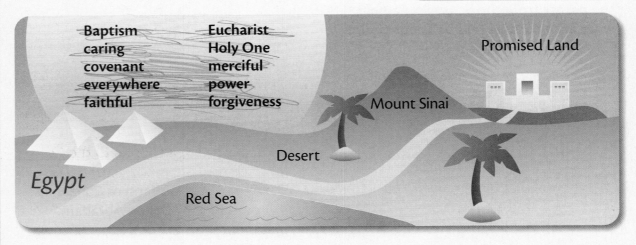

Baptism
caring
covenant
everywhere
faithful

Eucharist
Holy One
merciful
power
forgiveness

Promised Land

Mount Sinai

Desert

Egypt

Red Sea

1. God freed the Israelites from slavery and showed his great

   power .

2. God and his people were united in a

   holy _covenant_ .

3. We are united to God in a covenant

   by our _Baptism_ .

4. God always keeps his promises, so we say that he is

   faithful .

5. Jesus feeds us in a special way in the

   Eucharist .

6. God is always ready to forgive our sins.

   He is _merciful_ .

7. God fed his people in the desert. He is loving and

   caring .

8. We worship God because he is the

   Holy One .

9. In the Sacrament of Penance and Reconciliation we receive God's

   forgiveness .

10. God is present

    everywhere .

The Greatness and Goodness of God

Introduction

Leader: Let us begin our prayer with the Sign of the Cross.

All: In the name of the Father, and of the Son, and of the Holy Spirit.

Amen.

Leader: We have come to worship the Lord together. Let us sing to God with joy!

Song

Reading

Leader: Long ago God revealed his greatness and goodness in the wonderful things he did. He freed the Israelites from slavery and saved them from their enemies. He invited them to be his people and to let him guide them.

Reader: Give thanks to the LORD, call his name, proclaim his deeds to the people! Sing to him, sing his praises, tell about all his wondrous deeds! Glory in his holy name. Rejoice, O hearts, that seek the LORD!

adapted from Psalm 105:1–3

Psalm Prayer

Group 1: Sing joyfully to the LORD, all you lands.

Serve the LORD with gladness.

Come before him with joyful song.

Group 2: Know that the LORD is God. He made us.

We belong to him. We are his people, the sheep he tends.

Group 1: Give thanks to the LORD. Praise his holy name.

The LORD Yahweh is good.

Group 2: His kindness and his faithfulness never end.
adapted from Psalm 100

Song

Response

Leader: God cares for us with great love. He sent his Son to save us. Jesus stays with us. He feeds us with his own Body and Blood. Let us praise and thank God for his goodness to us.

Group 1: You care for all your children with love.

We give you thanks and praise!

Group 2: You feed us with the Bread of Life.

We thank you for this Living Bread!

Group 1: You dwell among us in your holy Church.

We want to stay close to you.

Group 2: You are faithful and true to your promises.

We trust you. We believe all you have said.

Group 1: You love us with an endless love.

We want to love you more, O LORD our God!

Group 2: You are so great and so good! We thank you for yourself!

Leader: O God Our Father, we have praised you in song and prayer. We also want to live out our worship by serving you in all our brothers and sisters. Help us to do this always. Amen.

Silent Prayer

Leader: Think of a special way in which you will try to serve God better today. Tell God about it. Ask him to help you.

(Pause for silent prayer.)

Conclusion

All: Our Father . . .

Leader: Let us bless the Lord.

All: Thanks be to God.

Family Feature

Merciful Acts

In Matthew 25:35–40, Jesus speaks to some righteous people. He tells them that acts of mercy, even the smallest kindnesses are holy and pleasing to God.

"For I was hungry and you gave me food, I was thirsty and you gave me drink, a stranger and you welcomed me, naked and you clothed me, ill and you cared for me, in prison and you visited me."

Then the righteous will answer him and say, "Lord, when did we see you hungry and feed you, or thirsty and give you drink? When did we see you a stranger and welcome you, or naked and clothe you? When did we see you ill or in prison, and visit you?"

And the king will say to them in reply, "Amen, I say to you, whatever you did for one of these least brothers of mine, you did for me."

Matthew 25:35–40

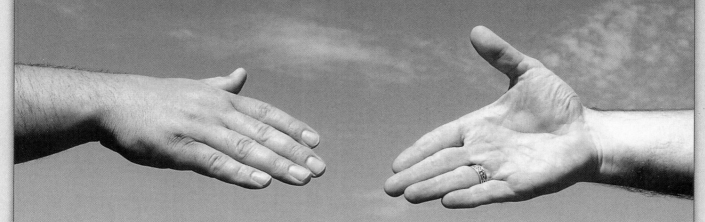

Family Feature

Mercy in Everyday Life

It is interesting that the righteous people were surprised to find out that their acts of kindness were important; they had shown love for its own sake. They had not realized that the Son of Man was present in every person who received their acts of mercy.

Parents do such acts of mercy every day. Raising children involves feeding the hungry, sheltering the homeless, clothing the naked, and visiting the sick. And those acts of mercy teach children how to show mercy themselves as they grow up and go out into the world.

The Corporal Works of Mercy

- Feed the hungry
- Give drink to the thirsty
- Clothe the naked
- Shelter the homeless
- Visit the sick
- Visit those in prison
- Bury the dead

These works of mercy flow from the Church's reflection on Scripture. The *Catechism of the Catholic Church* also notes that "Among all these, giving alms to the poor is one of the chief witnesses to fraternal charity: it is also a work of justice pleasing to God" (#2447).

Visit **www.ChristOurLife.org/family** for more family resources.

Our response to God's love is to show love.

Saint Ignatius of Loyola put it well when he wrote, "Love consists in sharing what one has and what one is with those one loves. Love ought to show itself in deeds more than in words." These merciful deeds do not need to be heroic or elaborate. Love is shown in ordinary actions, just as the ordinary objects and places in our home reveal the presence of God.

Whoever has two cloaks should share with the person who has none. And whoever has food should do likewise.

Luke 3:11

But as to what is within, give alms, and behold, everything will be clean for you.

Luke 11:41

If a brother or sister has nothing to wear and has no food for the day, and one of you says to them, "Go in peace, keep warm, and eat well," but you do not give them the necessities of the body, what good is it?

James 2:15–16

Be mindful of prisoners as if sharing their imprisonment, and of the ill-treated as of yourselves, for you also are in the body.

Hebrews 13:3

Pope John Paul II visits Mehmet Ali Agca, the man who attempted to assassinate him, in his cell at the Rebibbia Jail in Rome.

Family Feature

Acts of Mercy

For each of the Scripture passages, write an act of mercy your family can do together.

Luke 3:11

_____

Luke 11:14

_____

James 2:15–16

_____

Hebrews 13:3

_____

Write a prayer or choose another Scripture passage that inspires your family to act with mercy.

_____

_____

_____

_____

God's Plan Is a Plan of Love

. . . Jesus came to Galilee proclaiming the gospel of God:

"This is the time of fulfillment. The kingdom of God is at hand.

Repent, and believe in the gospel."

Mark 1:14–15

A Letter Home

Dear Parents and Family,

The lessons based on the Apostles' Creed continue in this unit with a focus on Jesus' coming, his work, and his teaching. The children will learn what God's kingdom is like, and they are invited to live the spirit of God's kingdom by loving others as Jesus has loved them.

The chapter "God Created People to Share His Life" explains that the first people fell from grace when they sinned and that, through sin, evil entered the world. The children will come to appreciate both the goodness of God and the evil of sin.

Chapter 11, "God Sent His Son to Live Among Us," presents several powerful ideas: that the Son of God took on our human nature; that he was conceived by the Virgin Mary through the power of the Holy Spirit, and that he was born into this world just like us in all things except sin. The children will review the Fourth Commandment (honor your father and your mother).

They will meet John the Baptist in Chapter 12, "Jesus Revealed the Kingdom of God." They will hear the story of Jesus' baptism and how Jesus overcame the temptations of the devil. The children will discover how Jesus proclaimed the kingdom by driving out evil spirits, working miracles, and teaching in parables. The children will explore ways to apply Jesus' teaching to the circumstances of their daily lives.

The chapter "Jesus Came to Give Life" explains how Jesus showed his power over sin and death when he restored life and health to those who both needed and desired it. The children will learn how Jesus' healing continues in the Sacrament of Penance and Reconciliation. They will also learn how to respond to his love by acting as instruments of his healing power.

The last chapter of this unit, "God's Kingdom Is a Kingdom of Love," teaches the children that true service to God includes keeping the commandments and loving others as Jesus has loved them. Loving others as Jesus loves us all will spread warmth and joy in your family and beyond.

Visit **www.ChristOurLife.org/family** for more family resources.

God Created People to Share His Life

We Have Natural Powers

God created all kinds of creatures—plants, minerals, and animals. God gave each creature its own special gifts and powers.

A redwood tree has the natural power to grow over 220 feet high. Some redwoods are 10 feet wide. Some have the power to live for more than 1,500 years!

Gold is a mineral. It has the natural power to be flattened out to less than .00001 of an inch. One ounce of gold can stretch out to a distance of over 50 miles!

Dogs have an amazing natural ability to smell things. They can sniff out all kinds of smells that we don't even notice. Dogs can use their natural power of smell to save people.

God created human beings in a very special way. The **Scriptures**, or holy writings collected in the Old and New Testaments, say that God created human beings in his own image and likeness, male and female. God made them equal.

He gave the human family special gifts. Humans have natural powers to think, choose, and love. No other creature has these natural powers.

Human beings are to work as partners to care for God's world and everyone in it.

Adam and Eve Shared in God's Life

God gave the first man and woman an even greater gift than human life. God gave them a share in his own life. It was a supernatural life. *Super-* means "above" or "greater." What do you think *supernatural* means?

extra special

Human beings received more than their natural human gifts. They received supernatural gifts. By sharing in God's life, they became God's own children so that they could enjoy his friendship. Adam and Eve could never do anything to deserve this. God gave them this gift freely, out of love. This sharing in God's life is called grace. *Grace* means "favor" or "gift."

Grace gives us the supernatural gifts of faith, **hope**, and **charity**. Faith is a gift of God that helps us believe in him. Hope is the gift of confidence in God. Charity means loving God first, then others, and oneself.

With these gifts we can believe in God, hope in his promises, and love him. We can see and enjoy God forever in heaven.

Our Life Is a Gift from God

What are some of the wonderful things you can do because you have life? What do you like most about being alive?

Draw a picture of you doing something that makes you feel alive.

The best thing about being alive is all my friend and family.

Sin Spoiled God's Plan for Us

A story in the Bible tells us that the **devil** wanted to destroy Adam and Eve's friendship with God. God had given them every good thing they could ever want. The only thing that was forbidden was the fruit of one special tree. The devil tempted Adam and Eve to disobey God's law and eat that fruit.

The devil made what God had forbidden seem good. Eve freely chose to turn against God. She listened to the devil and ate. Then she gave some to Adam, and he too chose to disobey God by eating. As soon as they had eaten the fruit, Adam and Eve felt ashamed.

Adam and Eve had turned from God's friendship. They lost the special gifts that had made them so happy. Their sin brought evil into the world. Before they sinned, Adam and Eve had never felt pain. There had been no suffering or death. Now evil would make them suffer. One day they would die.

This first sin spoiled God's plan of love. Now we are born in original sin. We have to struggle against evil. We sometimes desire to do sinful things. It is hard for us to choose what is truly good.

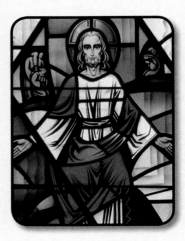

Jesus Is Our Redeemer

God still loved Adam and Eve. They had done wrong, but they were still his children. Because God loves us all, he promised a **Redeemer** to save all people from the power of sin and death. The Redeemer that God promised was his own Son, Jesus Christ. Through Jesus we can live a new life of grace.

All that Jesus did pleased God his Father. All that Jesus taught shows us the way to happiness here and forever in heaven.

Jesus is present with us. He gives us all we need to be united with God. He offers himself to his heavenly Father for our sins.

Jesus helps us grow in love for God our Father and others. He helps us be unselfish. He helps us forgive those who have hurt us. If we follow Jesus, we live in grace. We are freed from the power of sin.

Psalm Prayer

O LORD, our Lord,
    how awesome is your name through
        all the earth!
    You have set your majesty above the
        heavens!
When I see your heavens, the work of your
        fingers,
    the moon and stars that you set in
        place—
What are humans that you are mindful of
        them,
    mere mortals that you care for them?
Yet you have made them little less than a
        god,
    crowned them with glory and honor.
You have given them rule over the works of
        your hands,
    put all things at their feet:
All sheep and oxen,
    even the beasts of the field,
The birds of the air, the fish of the sea,
    and whatever swims the paths of the
        seas.

Psalm 8:2,4–9

A Moment with Jesus

Quietly pray to Jesus using the words of the Psalm Prayer. Write down some things that make God great.

he is greatful

he forgives

he cares

he loves

he helps

he made the world

he

Thank Jesus for sharing his grace with us.

Natural and Supernatural Powers

Write the missing words to finish the sentences below. Circle the answers in the puzzle.

1. We have natural powers to *choose*, *love*, and *think*.

2. Our share in God's life is called *grace*.

3. Grace means "favor" or "*gift*."

4. Supernatural powers are above our *natural* powers.

5. We have the supernatural powers to *hope* in God, to *believe* in God's promises, and to *love* God above all.

C	H	O	O	S	E
K	G	T	R	A	N
N	O	H	O	P	E
G	R	A	C	E	W
I	T	P	H	R	O
F	H	B	E	N	H
T	I	E	R	A	U
D	N	L	P	T	M
S	K	I	O	U	A
C	N	E	W	R	N
L	L	V	E	A	L
B	R	R	R	L	W

God Is Awesome

Pick your favorite words from the Psalm Prayer. Draw a picture to go with those words:

Supernatural Gifts

Match the word with its meaning.

faith — confidence in God

hope — a gift that helps us believe in God

charity — love of God and others

We Remember

What is grace?
Grace is sharing in God's life.

How was grace lost for all?
Grace was lost for all through the sin of our first parents.

Who overcame sin so we could have the gift of grace?
Jesus overcame sin so we could have the gift of grace.

What are three supernatural powers that grace gives human beings?
Grace gives human beings the supernatural powers of faith, hope, and charity.

Words to Know
charity   Redeemer
devil   Scriptures
hope

We Respond

I will thank Jesus for the gift of grace. When I find it hard to do something good, I will pray, "Jesus, help me."

Building Family Faith

CHAPTER SUMMARY The sin of Adam and Eve spoiled God's plan to have human beings share his supernatural life. Jesus redeemed us from sin, but we still must struggle against evil.

REFLECT
"Behold, now is a very acceptable time; behold, now is the day of salvation."
2 Corinthians 6:2

DISCUSS AS A FAMILY
- Talk about a time when you saw something that was wrong, and did something about it.
- Discuss your understanding of sin.
- Have you ever known the right thing to do and wanted to do it, but found it very hard to do so? Discuss.

PRAY
Come into our hearts, Lord Jesus. Give us the courage to do what is right.
DO
Have your child make a list of people with whom he or she has had disagreements. Pray for them at bedtime.

Visit **www.ChristOurLife.org/family** for more family resources.

God Sent His Son Jesus to Live Among Us

God Prepared the World for the Savior

When something important is going to happen, we prepare for it. How does your family prepare for Christmas?

One of the most important things that ever happened was the coming of Jesus on the first Christmas. Do you remember how God prepared the world for his Son? First, God chose a people from whom the Savior would come. He called Abraham to be the father of these people. God led them to know and to love him.

When God's people were slaves in Egypt, God called Moses to free them and to lead them to the Promised Land. He made a covenant of love with them and gave them his laws. Then God gave his people kings, like David. When the people forgot their

covenant, God sent prophets to call them back to him.

Finally, God chose Mary to be the mother of Jesus. God kept her free from original sin. He sent an angel to announce that she would be the mother of the Savior. Mary listened to God's message and said yes. When she and Joseph were married, Joseph became the foster father of God's own Son.

When Mary said yes, the Son of God became man through the power of the Holy Spirit. This is called the **Incarnation**. It is one of the main mysteries of our faith.

Circle the names of the people on this page who had a role in preparing for the Savior.

Jesus Was Born in a Stable in Bethlehem

According to God's plan, Caesar, the Roman emperor, ordered a census so that every person could be counted. The head of each family had to register in his hometown.

Joseph was from the family of David. He traveled from Nazareth to Bethlehem, the town of David. He went with Mary, his wife, who was soon to have a child.

Joseph and Mary stayed in a stable because there was no room for them in the inn. While they were there, Mary gave birth to a son. She wrapped him in swaddling clothes and laid him in a manger.

There were shepherds nearby, keeping watch over their flocks through the night. The angel of the Lord appeared to them, shining with the glory of the Lord. The shepherds were very much afraid, but the angel spoke to them. "Do not be afraid. I bring you good news of great joy that will be for all the people. Today in the city of David a savior has been born for you. He is Christ the Lord. Here is a sign for you: you will find a baby wrapped in swaddling clothes and lying in a manger."

Suddenly, there was with the angel a great number of heavenly spirits. They were praising God and saying:

"Glory to God in the highest, and peace to his people on earth."

The shepherds hurried away and found Mary and Joseph and the baby lying in a manger. They told what they had seen and heard. Then they praised God.

adapted from Luke 2:1–20

A Moment with Jesus

Quietly pray the words of the angels in Luke's story. Tell Jesus how happy you are that he was born.

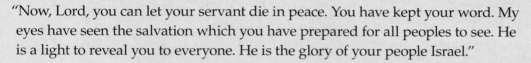

Simeon and Anna Recognized Jesus as the Light of the World

Jesus came as a light to lead all people back to God. He came to overcome the darkness of sin and to teach us truth. The story of the Presentation shows us how Simeon and Anna recognized Jesus as this light.

Mary and Joseph took the child Jesus to the Temple to present him to the Lord. An old man named Simeon knew the child was the light of the world. He was happy that he had lived to see the Savior.

Simeon took Jesus into his arms and praised God, saying:

> "Now, Lord, you can let your servant die in peace. You have kept your word. My eyes have seen the salvation which you have prepared for all peoples to see. He is a light to reveal you to everyone. He is the glory of your people Israel."
>
> adapted from Luke 2:29–32

Simeon told Mary that she would have much sorrow. Her son Jesus would suffer and die in his battle against evil. Mary would share in his sufferings.

An old woman named Anna was praying in the Temple. She was a prophetess. When she saw Jesus with Simeon, she gave thanks to God. Anna told the people waiting for the Savior what she had seen.

Jan Tillemans ,
Presentation of Jesus to Simeon

Jesus Honors His Mother and Father

When Jesus was a child, the people of Nazareth did not know that Jesus was the Savior, the Son of God. Jesus lived like any other Jewish boy. He was obedient and respectful to his parents and teachers. He played with the other children. He was kind and helpful to his neighbors. People knew him only as the son of Joseph and Mary. Jesus probably worked as a carpenter like Joseph until he was about 30 years old.

We learn an important truth from the childhood of Jesus: Through our ordinary actions we can give God our worship and love. We join our actions with those of Jesus and offer them to God. Then even our most ordinary actions become pleasing to God.

God our Father gave us the Fourth Commandment to help us make Jesus the Lord of our families. It tells us, "Honor and obey your parents."

Others besides our parents guide and protect us. When we respect and obey our leaders, we keep the Fourth Commandment and make Christ's light burn brightly.

Jesus Is Our Light

> "I am the light of the world. Whoever follows me will not walk in darkness, but will have the light of life."
>
> John 8:12

We are followers of Jesus. We follow his light. We can help make his light burn brightly wherever we are. We can make his light burn brightly in our own homes. Each member of a family can make Christ's light shine. Then everyone will see that Jesus is Lord of that family!

Honor Code

Use the Code Key to find five words that tell us how we honor our parents and keep Christ's light burning in our homes.

CODE KEY

1	2	3	4	5	6	7	8
E	L	O	P	R	S	T	Y

L O v e   O B E Y   H e l p
2 3 1   3 1 8   1 2 4

P R A Y   r e s p E c T
4 5 8   5 1 6 4 1 7

The Christmas Story

Match the words in the Word Bank with the following clues.

WORD BANK

Angel	Bethlehem
census	inn
Joseph	Jesus
manger	Mary
Nazareth	shepherds

1. Mother of Jesus _Mary_

2. Foster father of Jesus _Joseph_

3. Our Savior's name _Jesus_

4. One who announced the birth of Jesus _angel_

5. Holy Family's first visitors _shepherds_

6. Place where Mary laid Jesus _manger_

7. Place that had no room for Mary and Joseph _inn_

8. Reason Mary and Joseph went to Bethlehem _census_

9. City of David _Bethlehem_

10. Town where Joseph and Mary lived _Nazareth_

A Puzzle for You!

Unscramble the words and fill in the boxes with the letters in the right order.

1. Jesus shows us the way to eternal ELFI.

2. Jesus overcame the darkness of NIS.

3. Simeon said Jesus was the YRGOL of his people.

4. To follow Jesus is sometimes ADRH.

5. Jesus came to teach all people the HUTTR.

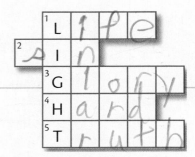

1. L i f e
2. S i n
3. G l o r y
4. H a r d
5. T r u t h

We Remember

What is the mystery of the Incarnation?
The mystery of the Incarnation is the Son of God becoming man through the power of the Holy Spirit.

How do we honor our parents?
We honor our parents when we love, obey, help, respect, and pray for them.

Word to Know
Incarnation

We Respond

I believe in Jesus Christ, the Son of God, who was born of the Virgin Mary!

I will keep the light of Christ burning brightly by obeying without complaining.

Building Family Faith

CHAPTER SUMMARY God became man in the person of Jesus. Jesus lived a fully human life. We can learn from him, imitate him, and follow him to heaven. Jesus is the light of the world.

REFLECT

And suddenly there was a multitude of the heavenly host with the angel, praising God and saying:
"Glory to God in the highest and on earth peace to those on whom his favor rests."
Luke 2:13–14

DISCUSS AS A FAMILY

• Jesus was part of a family. What would his parents have done for him? What would he have done for his parents?

• The angels sang with joy when Jesus came. How do we praise and honor Jesus?

• How is Jesus living among us today?

PRAY

Thank you, Jesus, for becoming human like us. Show us how to become more like you.

DO

Make a candle part of your family's celebration of Christmas. Place it on the dinner table. Talk about how the candle is a symbol of the light of Christ, which is burning brightly in your family.

Visit **www.ChristOurLife.org/family** for more family resources.

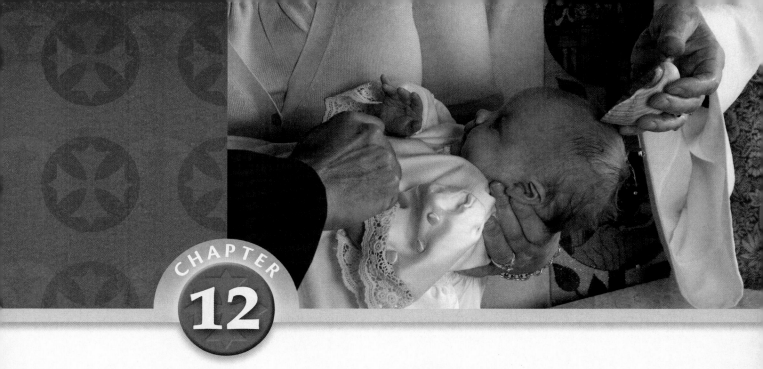

CHAPTER 12

Jesus Revealed the Kingdom of God

Jesus Begins His Public Mission

John the Baptist was sent by God to prepare people to receive Jesus and the **Kingdom of God**.

John preached to the people and baptized many in the Jordan River. This was not the Sacrament of Baptism as we know it. It was a baptism of sorrow for sin.

When Jesus left Nazareth to begin teaching, he came to John to be baptized. John recognized Jesus as the one for whom he had been preparing. So when Jesus went into the water, John tried to stop him.

John said "Do you come to me to be baptized? I need to be baptized by you." Jesus said to him, "Let us do this to fulfill what God wants." So John baptized Jesus.

Then God gave a sign of his love and approval of Jesus. As Jesus came out of the water, the heavens opened. The Spirit of God came down like a dove upon him. A voice came from heaven and said:

"This is my beloved Son. I am well pleased with him."

adapted from Matthew 3:13–17

Jesus is the all-holy **Son of God.** He did not need to be baptized. Jesus' baptism was a **Revelation** from God about who Jesus was and his mission from God the Father. Jesus was giving his life to the work his Father had sent him to do. With his baptism, Jesus began his public **mission** as the **Messiah,** the Savior.

Jesus Showed His Power over Satan

After his baptism Jesus was led by the Holy Spirit into the desert. For 40 days he fasted and prayed in order to prepare to do his Father's work.

Satan saw that Jesus was weak from hunger. He tempted Jesus to turn away from God's plan. He tempted Jesus to work wonders to prove that he was the Messiah. Satan also showed Jesus all the kingdoms that he could rule if he would worship Satan.

Jesus said no to Satan. Jesus answered Satan's temptations by showing love for his Father. Jesus chose to obey his Father's plan.

Satan always tries to destroy our friendship with God. He tries to draw us away from doing God's will. God does not force us to love him. He leaves us free. But God helps us overcome temptation if we ask him.

The Path of Life

Draw the path that avoids temptation.

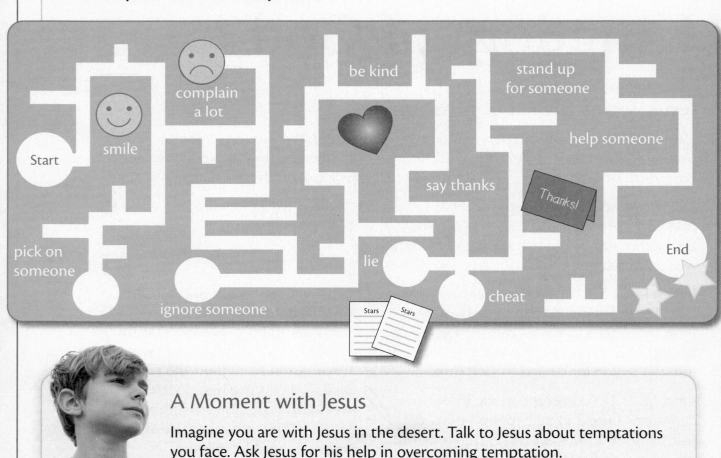

A Moment with Jesus

Imagine you are with Jesus in the desert. Talk to Jesus about temptations you face. Ask Jesus for his help in overcoming temptation.

Jesus Worked Miracles to Show the Kingdom Had Come

Jesus performed special works as signs that he had brought the Kingdom of God to earth. The Gospels call these wonderful deeds of Jesus miracles, or signs. Jesus' miracles helped people believe that he was the Messiah.

Some miracles showed power over nature. Jesus calmed storms at sea. Jesus also drove evil spirits out of people. His power over demons was a sign that he was the Savior who would overcome evil. Wherever Jesus rules, sin is driven out. Jesus brings his goodness, love, and happiness to those who open their hearts to him.

Jesus Told Parables About the Kingdom of God

Jesus revealed the Kingdom of God in his preaching. He taught by **parables,** or stories. In his parables, Jesus compared the Kingdom of God to everyday things the people saw or did. The parables made them think.

Have you ever seen a mustard seed? Jesus taught a parable about this seed:

"The kingdom of God is like a mustard seed, which is the smallest of all seeds. . . . But it grows to become the largest of plants, sending out branches for the birds of the sky to live in its shade."

adapted from Mark 4:30–32

Jesus was telling the people that God's kingdom would begin small but would grow into something great. The Church belongs to the Kingdom of God. People of every nation have become members of the Church. When we pray, make sacrifices, and love as Jesus did, the Church grows.

Jesus also shared a parable that tells us the great value of God's kingdom:

"Again, the kingdom of heaven is like a merchant searching for fine pearls. When he finds a pearl of great price, he goes and sells all that he has and buys it."

Matthew 13:45–46

God's kingdom within us is the life of grace. It is such a priceless gift that we could never pay enough to get it. To keep it safe is worth any sacrifice. God's kingdom is also in heaven. No earthly treasure can compare with what God has for us there.

Fill in the missing words.

Jesus taught using stories called __ __ __ __ __ __ __ __ .

He told us that God's kingdom grows like a __ __ __ __ __ __ __ seed.

The Kingdom of God is like a fine __ __ __ __ __ .

We Spread God's Kingdom in Different Ways

Good Christians love and serve God in all they do. With their talents they bring God's love to others in many ways. They bring the Spirit of Jesus to whatever they do. Can you tell how these people are spreading God's kingdom?

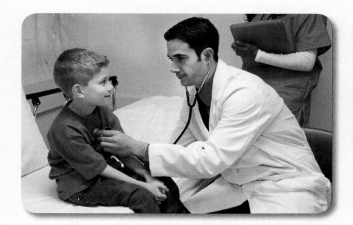

Keys to the Kingdom

Match the answers in the Word Bank with the following questions.

WORD BANK

A. baptism   D. parables
B. evil spirits   E. temptations
C. John   F. miracles

_____ **1.** What were the stories Jesus told about the kingdom?

_____ **2.** What were the signs Jesus worked to show the kingdom had come?

_____ **3.** What did Jesus show power over as a sign that his kingdom of goodness will win?

_____ **4.** What was a sign that Jesus was starting his public mission?

_____ **5.** How did Satan try to draw Jesus away from God's plan?

_____ **6.** Who baptized Jesus?

We Remember

What must we do to receive the Kingdom of God in our hearts?
To receive the Kingdom of God in our hearts, we listen to Jesus and let our lives be guided by his teaching.

How can we help the Church grow?
We can help the Church grow by praying, making sacrifices, and loving as Jesus did.

Words to Know

Kingdom of God	Revelation
Messiah	Satan
mission	Son of God
parable	

We Respond

Jesus, I want to help bring about your kingdom. Help me to be more loving and to help those in need.

Building Family Faith

CHAPTER SUMMARY The Kingdom of God arrived in our world when Jesus came. We spread this kingdom through our efforts to love and serve God and our fellow human beings.

REFLECT
Again, the kingdom of heaven is like a merchant searching for fine pearls. When he finds a pearl of great price, he goes and sells all that he has and buys it.

Matthew 13:45–46

DISCUSS AS A FAMILY
• How does our family love and serve others? What more could we do?
• What are the most difficult things we do? Why do we do them? Are they worth the sacrifice?

• Jesus says that the Kingdom of God is something we can't live without. What is our most precious possession?

PRAY
Our Father, who art in heaven, hallowed be thy name. Thy kingdom come, thy will be done, on earth as it is in heaven.

DO
As a family, choose something you can do to love and serve others.

Visit **www.ChristOurLife.org/family** for more family resources.

Jesus Came to Give Life

Jesus Cured the Man with Leprosy

In the time of Jesus, no one wanted to go near those who had leprosy because they were afraid of the disease. Lepers often had to leave their homes and live apart from other people.

> One day a man with leprosy came to Jesus and knelt before him. "Lord," he begged, "if you want to, you can cure me." Moved with pity, Jesus stretched out his hand and touched him. "I will do it," he said. "Be cured!" At once the leprosy left the man, and he was cured.
>
> adapted from Mark 1:40–42

The Gospel tells us that Jesus cured many lepers. Then they could begin a new life among their people.

What Jesus did for them is a sign of what he wants to do for us. Jesus wants to remove anything that separates us from God and his people. Jesus came to bring us the new life of grace and to make us one in his family—the Church.

When Jesus healed the man, he also healed his community. He returned the man to them. Sin does to us what people did to the man. It keeps us away from others and from God. It weakens us. It makes us less able to use our gifts for the good of God's family.

In the Sacrament of Penance and Reconciliation, Jesus heals us of sin by forgiving us. When we bring our sins to him and ask his pardon and help, he makes us one with God and one another.

Jesus Brought Life to the Widow's Son

Jesus was on his way to the city of Nain with his disciples. As they came near the city gate, a dead man was being carried out. He was an only son, and his mother was a widow.

Jesus' heart was filled with pity for this mother. "Do not cry," he said to her. Then he touched the coffin, and those carrying the body stopped. Jesus said, "Young man, I tell you, arise!" The dead man sat up and began to speak. Jesus gave him back to his mother.

Everyone was filled with awe and praised God, saying, "God has visited his people."

adapted from Luke 7:11–16

The Cure of the Blind Man

Reader 1: The signs Jesus worked showed that the Kingdom of God had come.

Reader 2: As Jesus came to Jericho, a blind man was begging at the side of the road. He could hear that a crowd was passing by.

Blind Man: What is happening?

Crowd: Jesus of Nazareth is passing by.

Blind Man: Jesus, Son of David, have pity on me!

Crowd: Be quiet! Don't make a scene!

Reader 3: But the man would not be quiet. He only cried out all the more.

Blind Man: Jesus, Son of David, help me. Have pity on me!

Reader 4: Jesus heard the man shouting to him. He stopped and stood still.

Jesus: Bring the man here to me.

Reader 5: They led the blind man to Jesus.

Jesus: What do you want me to do for you?

Blind Man: Lord, please let me see!

Jesus: Have sight. Your faith has saved you.

Reader 6: That very moment, the man was able to see. He began to follow Jesus, giving glory to God.

Blind Man: Praise God! I can see! I can see!

Crowd: Praise God!

adapted from Luke 18:35–43

Jesus Gave Life to a 12-Year-Old Girl and Healed a Woman

Reader 1: When Jesus returned to Galilee, a crowd of people welcomed him. An official of the synagogue came forward. He knelt before Jesus.

Jairus: Lord, please come to my house. My only daughter is dying. She is only 12 years old.

Reader 2: Jesus went with him. On the way, a woman with a terrible illness touched Jesus' coat. Her sickness was instantly cured.

Jesus: Someone has touched me.

Woman: I did, and I have been healed.

Jesus: My daughter, your faith has saved you. Go in peace.

Reader 2: Then a messenger arrived.

Messenger: Jairus, I'm so sorry. Your daughter is dead.

Jesus: Do not be afraid, Jairus. Just have faith, and she will be saved.

Reader 3: At the house, everyone was sad and crying because the child had died.

Jesus: Do not be sad any longer. She is not dead, but sleeping.

Reader 4: They all thought Jesus was foolish. They knew she was really dead. Then Jesus took the girl's hand.

Jesus: Child, arise!

Reader 6: The girl began breathing again. She immediately got up. Jesus told her parents to give her something to eat. Everyone was amazed. The girl's parents got their daughter back.

adapted from Luke 8:40–56

A Moment with Jesus

Imagine that Jesus takes your hand. What does he say to you? Thank Jesus for caring so much for children.

We Respect and Protect Life

Jesus brought life to many people.

He did this in many ways:

- teaching and being friends with people
- forgiving people of their sins and encouraging them to do good
- healing people of sickness or hurts
- bringing people back to life

Jesus showed us how important life is. He taught us to respect and protect human life. Through the Holy Spirit, Jesus gives us gifts to help us respect and protect life.

How are these children showing respect and protecting life?

What are some ways that you show how important life is?

CHAPTER 13 Review

Complete the sentences, using the words in the Word Bank.

faith   life
Messiah   ~~sin~~
Word

1. The miracles of Jesus show he was the _Messiah_ .

2. Jesus heals people from _sin_ .

3. We need open ears to hear God's _word_ .

4. Jesus told Jairus and us to have _faith_ .

5. Jesus gave back _life_ to the widow's son and to Jairus' daughter.

We Remember

What did Jesus say about anyone who believes in him?

Jesus said,

"I am the resurrection and the life; whoever believes in me, even if he dies, will live . . . "

John 11:25

We Respond

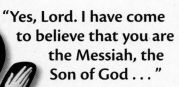

"Yes, Lord. I have come to believe that you are the Messiah, the Son of God . . . "

John 11:27

Building Family Faith

CHAPTER SUMMARY Jesus cured people and brought them back to life as a sign of the new life he brings to us. By loving and serving others, we imitate Jesus in his healing work.

REFLECT

Go and tell John what you have seen and heard: the blind regain their sight, the lame walk, lepers are cleansed, the deaf hear, the dead are raised, the poor have the good news proclaimed to them.

Luke 7:22

DISCUSS AS A FAMILY

• Jesus wants to heal what is broken in our minds, hearts, and bodies. What do we need to have healed? What needs to be healed in our family?

• What needs to be healed in the lives of people outside our family—our neighbors, children at school, or people in our parish?

PRAY

Lord Jesus, strengthen us. Heal us. Send new life to our family.

DO

Ask each family member to do one thoughtful or generous thing this week for someone who is sad or lonely. Consider what that person would like best and what each member of the family is best able to do.

Visit **www.ChristOurLife.org/family** for more family resources.

God's Kingdom Is a Kingdom of Love

Jesus Taught Us About the Spirit of the Kingdom

Jesus taught us that the spirit of God's kingdom is a spirit of generous, loving service. God's plan is for us to love one another.

Jesus' teaching about God's kingdom is in the Sermon on the Mount in Matthew's

Gospel. In it Jesus teaches the disciples and crowds about serving God's kingdom.

The Teachings of Jesus

Read the following teachings of Jesus and think about them. Write the number of the message that matches each sentence in the box.

1. "You know that the law says, 'You shall not kill.' But I tell you this: You shall not be angry with your brother at all. If you are bringing your gift to the altar and remember that your brother has something against you, go first and make up with your brother. Then come and offer your gift."

    adapted from Matthew 5:21–24

2. "If someone tells you to carry a load for one mile, offer to carry it for two miles. And if someone asks for something from you, give him what he asks. Do not turn your back on a person who wants to borrow from you."

    adapted from Matthew 5:41–42

3. "Love your enemies. Pray for people who do you wrong. In this way you will be children of your heavenly Father. He makes the sun rise on the bad and the good. Be perfect, just as your heavenly Father is perfect. Do to others whatever you would like them to do to you."

    adapted from Matthew 5:44–48; 7:12

_____ Share generously what you have.

_____ Forgive those who hurt you.

_____ Love everyone even if they have hurt you.

A Check for Service

Read these sentences. Check (✓) each one that tells a way to spread God's kingdom by serving and loving others.

_____ 1. Work hard so you can use your talents to make others happy.

_____ 2. Pray for the needs of others.

_____ 3. Make others feel they are not as good as you are.

_____ 4. Refuse to join others in using curse words.

_____ 5. Offer your help even before you are asked.

_____ 6. Boss others around.

_____ 7. Sacrifice some of your money to give to the missions.

_____ 8. Act as if you are better than someone else.

_____ 9. Do jobs at home and at school carefully and cheerfully.

_____ 10. Do something to cheer up someone who is sick or lonely.

Planning to Grow

Think of Jesus, the light of the world. He wants you to please his Father and help spread his light all over the world. Write two ways you plan to do this.

1. _____

_____

_____

2. _____

_____

_____

_____

Who's Who in Your Life?

List some of the people who have brought you closer to Jesus.

_____

_____

_____

_____

We Remember

How do we spread the Kingdom of God?
We spread the Kingdom of God by loving and forgiving one another and by living as sisters and brothers.

We Respond

Father, hallowed be your name, your kingdom come.

Luke 11:2

Checking Up on the Unit

Check (✓) the right ending for each sentence.

1. God created human beings because

   __✗__ he wanted to share his life and happiness with them.

   _____ he needed them for his happiness.

2. After Adam and Eve sinned,

   _____ God no longer loved them.

   __✗__ God still loved them and promised to help them.

3. The Redeemer whom God sent

   __✗__ was his own Son born of the Virgin Mary.

   _____ had to be baptized because of his sin.

4. The special signs Jesus worked to reveal the Kingdom of God are called

   _____ parables.

   __✗__ miracles.

5. By healing the sick, Jesus showed that he had come to

   _____ rid the world of sickness and pain.

   __✗__ heal people of separation from community and God.

6. Jesus worked miracles to

   __✗__ reveal that he was the Messiah.

   _____ force people to believe in him.

7. Some people did not believe in Jesus because they were expecting

   _____ a spiritual kingdom.

   __✗__ an earthly Messiah.

Who's Who?

Write the letter of the answer on each line.

A. the blind man   D. John the Baptist
B. the leper   E. Satan
C. Jesus   F. Jairus's daughter

B 1. Who was pushed out of the community because of a disease?

A 2. Who called out for help and was cured at once by Jesus?

F 3. Who did Jesus bring back from the dead?

E 4. Who tried to turn Jesus away from doing his Father's will?

C 5. Who taught that serving God means obeying his laws with a true and generous love?

D 6. Who told the people to change their hearts and prepare for the coming of the Savior?

What's the Parable?

Write the answers to the questions on the lines.

1. In which parable did Jesus say that the Kingdom of God would be small at first but would grow into something great?

   Mustard Seed

2. In which parable did Jesus teach us that God's kingdom is more valuable than anything else?

   The pwsl

Word Find

Find words that name things you can use to help spread God's kingdom. (Words go across and down.) Circle them and be ready to tell how you could use each one to help and serve others.

```
P T R P O S K A T E S
E I B I K E N B O O K
A M I C I T O Y S M T
C E A L L O W A N C E
E F O O D O L Q S W P
G R N T A L E N T S A
A V T H R S D J O Y P
M O N E Y Z G H O M E
E M U S I C E F U N R
```

We Pray for the Coming of God's Kingdom

Leader: Let us begin our prayer with the Sign of the Cross.

All: In the name of the Father, and of the Son, and of the Holy Spirit.

Amen.

Song

Readings

Leader: God invites all of us to live in his kingdom. If we believe in Jesus and open our hearts to his works, he will free us from the power of sin. He will give us peace and joy in this life. He will bring us to the kingdom of his Father, where we will enjoy eternal life. Let us listen to what Jesus tells us to do.

Reader 1: Give to anyone who asks and, if anyone wants to borrow, do not turn away.

Reader 2: Love your enemies.

Reader 3: Pray for people who hurt you.

Reader 4 Do to others what you would like them to do to you.

adapted from
Matthew 5:44; 7:12

All: Jesus, gentle and humble of heart, make our hearts like yours!

Leader: Lord, we have heard your Word. Help us accept it and show our love by what we do.

Song

Presentation of Gifts

(Place on the table your promise of good deeds as a sign that you want to follow Jesus.)

Leader: God our Father, we have praised you in song and prayer. We have shown that we want to serve you in all our sisters and brothers. Help us do this today and every day.

All: Amen.

Song

Leader: Let us bless the Lord.

All: Thanks be to God.

Sacrifices for God's Kingdom

Color a cross when you make a sacrifice to bring about God's kingdom.

Family Rituals

Every family has its rituals. The rituals may be as simple as where people tend to sit when watching TV together, or as elaborate as a Thanksgiving feast complete with favorite recipes handed down through the generations. Meals together, bedtime rituals, regular weekend outings, holidays, and special celebrations—these things are the glue that binds us together in our homes.

Young children especially love rituals. Rituals and routines provide a strong and reliable foundation as they begin to explore more of the world. Family rituals tell the family's story, revealing who we are and where we belong. Through them, children learn what is important.

Family rituals are also powerful ways to convey our faith and values to our children. Our characters are shaped by what we do over and over again. Our children's sense of who God is will be formed by family rituals, and so it's well worth giving careful thought to what these things are.

Family Feature

Build on the rituals you already have.

You already have many rituals, and they all mean something to your children. What do you do together at the beginning and end of each day? How do you spend the weekends? How does your family approach Sunday Mass? What do you do at holidays? Which of these rituals work best and which need to be changed?

See the sacred in the ordinary.

Most rituals involve commonplace things, such as eating food, taking a walk, saying hello and goodbye, and relaxing together. When we allow faith to guide our vision, these everyday activities can become revelations of God's mercy, love, and generosity. Children are naturally drawn to the sacred. Parents just need to point them in the right direction.

Share meals together.

The family meal is probably the most powerful ritual of all. It's the anchor of the day. Dinnertime is the time to share the events of the day, along with good food, conversation, and the pleasure of one another's company. Commit to sit down and eat together at least five times a week.

Make bedtime special.

Make a ritual out of saying goodnight to your children. The coming of night and  the need to sleep can cause anxiety in many children. This is a time for loving, secure time with mom and dad. Pray together. Read a story. Tuck your child in. Say, "I love you."

Mark comings and goings.

Give your child a loving sendoff in the morning. Welcome your child home with a big hello. In some homes, parents quickly trace the sign of the Cross on the child's forehead before he or she heads out the door—a lovely custom conveying their love and prayers for safety all day.

Celebrate the feasts.

The great Christian feasts are rich opportunities for families to develop rituals that convey a deep sense of faith and trust in God. Many are well established: the Advent wreath and its four candles, the Christmas tree and the manger scene, giving up things for Lent, or serving special foods at Easter. Develop your own special rituals as a good way to make these celebrations yours.

Visit **www.ChristOurLife.org/family** for more family resources.

The Light of Christ

Write the name of a family member or other loved person on each candle. As you "light" the candle by drawing a flame on the wick, say the following prayer:

> Lord, thank you for (Name). Bless and keep him/her.
>
> In your name we pray.
>
> Amen.

Family Feature

Make a decorative candleholder

- Wash and dry a clear glass jelly jar or drinking glass.

- Choose one of the symbols of Christ on this page. You can trace the image and color it, or clip the image directly from the page.

- Cut a piece of clear contact paper or invisible tape that is a little bit bigger than the image you have chosen.

- Place the decorated side of your image on the sticky side of the contact paper or tape.

- Use scissors to trim the contact paper or tape to fit the contours of the image, leaving about a half inch of sticky border.

- Stick the image onto the glass.

- Place a votive or tea light candle in the holder and light carefully.

Jesus Brings Us to the Kingdom of God

Jesus humbled himself, becoming obedient to death, even death on a cross. Because of this, God greatly honored him and gave him the name that is above every name. At the name of Jesus every knee should bend and every tongue confess that Jesus Christ is Lord, to the glory of God the Father.

adapted from Philippians 2:8–11

A Letter Home

Dear Parents and Family,

It's at the heart of our faith—the Paschal Mystery. Unit 4 explores this mystery, walking your child through the Lord's passion, death, Resurrection, and ascension into glory. Jesus' sacrifice exemplified his tremendous love and generosity. As members of the Church, we share in the Paschal Mystery and are called to demonstrate that love and generosity in serving God and others.

In the first chapter of Unit 4, the children will learn that Jesus chose to suffer and die for us, sacrificing his own life to save us. This sacrifice constitutes the New Covenant between God and his people, which we celebrate at Mass. The children will discover that following Jesus helps give meaning and comfort to those who suffer.

Chapter 16 explains that Jesus destroyed death and restored our opportunity to live a life of grace through his Resurrection. Jesus frees us from our fears and brings us peace. The children will learn that while it's hard to lose a loved one, death is a gateway to eternal life. This belief can offer your family great comfort and hope in such a situation.

Jesus' ascension into heaven is the focus of Chapter 17. The children learn that Jesus will come again in glory to judge all people on how well we have observed his law of love.

In Chapter 18, the children learn that Jesus kept his promise to send the Holy Spirit. They will hear about Pentecost, when the Holy Spirit descended on the apostles and disciples of Jesus. The Holy Spirit continues to be with us, helping us to carry on the work of Jesus.

Unit 4 concludes with a discussion of Mary's Assumption and her role as queen of heaven and earth. The children also are introduced to the Communion of Saints, the family of God whose members support and pray for one another. As you support and pray for one another in your own family, you provide a living example of the family of God to your child.

At the end of each chapter in this unit, the children will bring home a review of the chapter along with the Building Family Faith feature, which will give you a quick review of what your child has learned. At the end of the unit, the children will bring home the Family Feature handout to help nurture the family's faith at home.

Visit **www.ChristOurLife.org/family** for more family resources.

CHAPTER 15

Jesus Suffered and Died for Us

Jesus Was Honored as King

On the Sunday before he died, Jesus rode into Jerusalem. The people welcomed him as a king. They spread their clothes and palm branches on the road. They called him the Son of David and shouted,

> "Hosanna!
>   Blessed is he who comes in the name of the Lord!"
>
> Mark 11:9

The people thought Jesus would be the great leader who would free them from Roman rule. Jesus accepted the joyful praise of the people. This was his victory march. Soon he would win the victory over sin and death.

On Palm Sunday, we carry blessed palms and proclaim that Jesus is king of heaven and earth. We greet him as the Redeemer, who overcame sin and death by giving up his life and then rising to glory.

103

Jesus Made a New Covenant

At a Passover meal the Israelites celebrated how God had freed them from slavery in Egypt. They renewed their covenant by promising to keep God's commandments and to live as his Chosen People. They offered a Passover lamb in sacrifice.

Jesus celebrated the Passover meal with his apostles the night before he died. At this meal Jesus made a New Covenant with them and us. He gave us a new commandment. He offered himself as the lamb who saves us from sin and death. By his power, bread and wine became his Body and Blood. He offered them to God as he would offer himself on the cross. Then he gave himself to his disciples under the forms of bread and wine.

Today Jesus continues to make his sacrifice present in the **Sacrifice of the Mass.** At Mass we celebrate the New Covenant. It is also our covenant meal celebrated and shared by God's holy people.

Write the law of the New Covenant by printing above each letter the one that comes before it in the alphabet.

as I have loved you
B T J I B W F M P W F E Z P V

so you also should
T P Z P V B M T P T I P V M E

Love one another
M P W F   P O F B O P U I F S

John 13:34

Jesus Faced His Agony

On the night before he died, Jesus went with Peter, James, and John to the garden of Gethsemane. He told them, "My soul is filled with sorrow. Wait here, and keep awake!"

Jesus was truly human. Like all people, he did not want to suffer or die. In fear he fell to the ground and prayed to his Father to save him from that hour. "My Father!" he said, "Everything is possible for you. Take this cup away from me, but not what I will but what you will."

Jesus went back to the apostles, but they were asleep. He said to Peter, "Are you asleep? Couldn't you stay awake one hour with me? Watch and pray that you may not be put to the test." The apostles did not know what to say.

Jesus left them and went away again to pray. He came back a second and a third time. Each time the apostles were sleeping. Then he said to them, "The hour has come. Get up! Let us go! My betrayer is near."

adapted from Mark 14:32–42

Jesus Gave His Life for Us

Jesus spent his whole life helping people and following God. He had told his disciples that he would suffer and die. Now the time had come.

While Jesus was in the garden of Gethsemane, Judas came with soldiers to arrest him. He kissed Jesus as a sign that the men should capture him. The apostles ran away in fear. Jesus was taken away to be questioned by the high priest. At the high priest's house, some of the guards hit Jesus and called him names.

The next day Jesus was sent to Pontius Pilate, the Roman governor. Pilate questioned Jesus. Pilate's soldiers whipped and bullied him. To make fun of Jesus, they made a crown of thorns to put on his head.

Pilate knew Jesus was not guilty of any crime. But the people who had gathered in the courtyard had turned against Jesus and demanded that he be crucified. Pilate gave in and sent Jesus outside the gates of Jerusalem to be crucified.

Jesus had to carry his cross the whole way. All along the way, people laughed at him. When they got to a hill called Calvary, Jesus was crucified.

At noon, darkness fell over the whole land. At three o'clock in the afternoon, Jesus cried out: "It is finished! Father, into your hands I entrust my spirit!" Jesus bowed his head and died.

A soldier guarding Jesus was amazed. He said, "Truly this man was the Son of God."

adapted from Mark 14:43–46; 15:1–39;
Matthew 27:15–44; Luke 23:1–5; John 19:2–6

We Take Up Our Cross

Jesus said that if we wish to follow him, we must take up our cross. This means accepting hard things that come into our lives. We may fail in things we try to do. Some people may hurt us. Things that happen may disappoint us or make us sad. When sufferings like these come, we can pray and ask Jesus to help us accept them as he did. Then he will use these sufferings to help others and to bring us closer to him.

Jesus promised that those who suffer with him will be with him in heaven. He will share his glory with those who have shared his cross. We can be happy with Jesus no matter what happens. We know that our sufferings can lead us to eternal happiness with God.

A Moment with Jesus

Think about all Jesus did to save us. Thank Jesus for his great love for us.

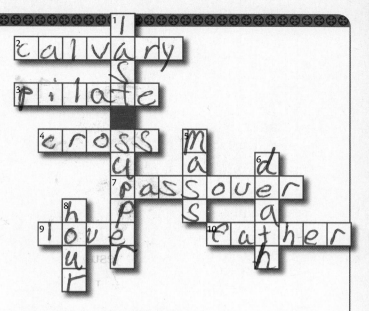

Jesus' Passion and Death

Complete the crossword.

Across

2. The hill where Jesus was crucified was _____ .

3. The governor who gave Jesus over to the soldiers was _____ .

4. The sign of Jesus' death is a _____ .

7. Jesus celebrated the Jewish feast of _____ .

9. By his death Jesus showed his great _____ .

10. Jesus prayed to his _____ .

Down

1. Jesus' final meal with his apostles is called the _____ _____ .

5. We celebrate Jesus' sacrifice when we are at _____ .

6. Jesus saved us by his suffering and _____ .

8. Jesus was disappointed when his apostles couldn't keep awake for an _____ .

The Places of the Passion

Find the places where Jesus prayed and suffered. Write the number in the correct circle. Then trace the journey of Jesus.

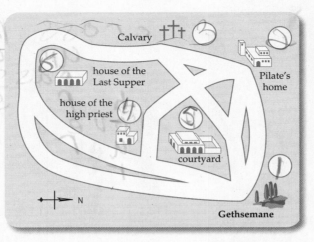

Calvary

house of the Last Supper

house of the high priest

Pilate's home

courtyard

N

Gethsemane

1. Garden where Jesus prayed
2. Home of the Roman governor
3. Place where Jesus was crucified
4. Place where Jesus was questioned
5. Place where the people gathered
6. Place where Jesus ate with his apostles

We Remember

What is the sacrifice of the New Covenant?
The sacrifice of the New Covenant is the Mass.

What is the law of the New Covenant?
The law of the New Covenant is "As I have loved you, so also should you love one another."

Why did Jesus willingly accept suffering and death?
Jesus willingly accepted suffering and death to save us from sin and death because he loved the Father and us.

Words to Know
Sacrifice of the Mass

We Respond

We adore you, O Christ, and we praise you, because by your holy cross you have redeemed the world.

Building Family Faith

CHAPTER SUMMARY By suffering and dying, Jesus broke the power of evil in our world. His death was also a lesson in how to love. When we suffer, we can remember and imitate his love.

REFLECT
This is my commandment: love one another as I love you. No one has greater love than this, to lay down one's life for one's friends.
John 15:12–13

DISCUSS AS A FAMILY
• Discuss how Jesus' suffering and death were acts of love. Do we find it difficult to see them as love?
• What burdens are people in our family carrying now? How can we give one another comfort?

PRAY
O my God, I love you above all things with my whole heart and soul, because you are good and worthy of all my love. I love my neighbor as myself for the love of you. I forgive all who have injured me, and I ask pardon of those whom I have injured. Amen.

DO
• Pray a decade of the Rosary as a family for friends, family, and neighbors who are suffering.

Visit **www.ChristOurLife.org/family** for more family resources.

Jesus Is Risen

The Risen Jesus Brings Peace and Joy

All of us have fears. Some fears are good because they keep us from harm. Other fears are not good when they keep us from feeling good about ourselves or from loving Jesus or others.

Mark an X before each fear you think is real for children your age.

_____ fear they won't have friends

_____ fear someone they love will die

_____ fear of the dark

_____ fear their parents don't love them

_____ fear of dogs

_____ fear someone might ask them to do something hurtful

_____ fear of reading out loud

_____ fear older children will beat them up

_____ fear their parents will be divorced

_____ fear they will lose their friends if they disagree with them

_____ fear of a terrorist attack

Jesus wants us to remember that he is always with us. He wants us to trust in his love and care. When we feel afraid, we can say, "Jesus, I trust in your loving care." Then we can face our fears and let love grow in our hearts.

The Disciples See the Risen Jesus

Early on the first day of the week after Jesus was crucified, Mary of Magdala and her friends found his tomb empty. Stories spread quickly. "His body has been stolen!" "He has risen and is alive!" What was the truth?

In the evening the disciples were gathered together behind locked doors. They were afraid of the people who had killed Jesus. Some disciples said that they had seen Jesus. They knew that he had been dead, but now he was alive. It sounded impossible! If he were alive, what did it mean?

Suddenly Jesus came and stood among them. He said, "Peace be with you" and showed them his hands and his side. The disciples were filled with joy when they saw the Lord. He said again, "Peace be with you. As the Father has sent me, so I send you."

After saying this, he breathed on them and said: "Receive the holy Spirit. Whose sins you forgive are forgiven them."

adapted from John 20:19–23

Jesus' Disciples Bring His Peace

After Jesus appeared to them, the disciples knew that Jesus was truly the Lord. He had come to take away all their fears. They were filled with hope and peace. The disciples would spread the good news that Jesus was risen. He had restored the eternal life of grace that had been lost by sin. Through them, he would forgive sins. Then the disciples would bring his peace to people everywhere.

Sadako Worked for Peace

The girl in the picture is Sadako Sasaki. She lived in Hiroshima, Japan. Her city was destroyed by a bomb in World War II. Many people were hurt, including Sadako.

She and her family prayed for people who were killed or hurt in the war. They worked for peace.

People all over the world heard about Sadako's prayers for peace. Because of her they wanted to work and pray for peace too.

Because of Sadako, the folded paper crane has become an international symbol of peace.

We Work for Peace

Everyone who works for peace helps build a better world. Christians are called to go out and bring Jesus' peace to the ends of the earth.

How can you bring Jesus' message of peace to your family and other people you meet?

A Moment with Jesus

Pray these words adapted from the Peace Prayer of Saint Francis.

Lord, make me an instrument of your peace:
where there is hatred, let me bring love;
where there is injury, let me bring pardon;
where there is doubt, let me bring faith;
where there is despair, let me bring hope;
where there is darkness, let me bring light;
and where there is sadness, let me bring joy.

We Celebrate Easter

Easter is the day we celebrate Jesus' Resurrection. It is the greatest feast of the whole year. It is Christ's great victory over sin and death. This victory is so great that we celebrate it every Sunday. We have a special eucharistic celebration this first day of the week. It should be a day of joy, relaxation, and peace. This is our response to all that Jesus has done for us.

Sunday is a day of celebration for all who follow Jesus.

How are the families in these pictures making Sunday special?

List two things your family likes to do to celebrate Sunday.

1. My family and I have diner together.

2. My family and I go to church together.

Jesus' Death Brought New Life

The beautiful Easter candle that is lighted at the Easter Vigil is called the paschal candle. It reminds us that Jesus, the light of the world, is still with us. We share in the light of this candle. It is a sign that we also share in Jesus' victory over sin and death.

Why then do people still die? Jesus' victory changed death to life. When we die, we live a new life in heaven.

Jesus has prepared a place in heaven for each of us. He has promised that if we love him, we will live with him forever and be perfectly happy. We do not fully understand what that means, but we can trust God. God keeps his word.

Jesus revealed something of the heavenly kingdom to John. In the last book of the Bible, John tells us:

> I heard a loud voice saying, "This is God's home with the human race! He will live among them and they will be his people. God will always be with them as their God. He will wipe every tear from their eyes. There shall be no more death or sorrow, crying or pain, for the old order has passed away."
>
> adapted from Revelation 21:3–4

When we die, we will live with Jesus in heaven. Jesus will come and take us to our new home. There we will be perfectly happy with God who loves us so much!

Death Is a Time of Sadness and Joy

If death is such a wonderful event, why are we sad when someone dies?

We are sad when someone dies because we miss the person we have loved. Jesus was sorrowful when his friend Lazarus died. He went to the place where Lazarus was buried, and he cried. The people knew that Jesus loved Lazarus and missed him. Jesus shows us that it is all right to be sad when someone we love dies.

Death is a time when we can be both happy and sad. We can be happy because through death, we go home to God. We will know and love God in a new way in heaven. We will see God's goodness and beauty. We will be filled forever with a joy greater than we can ever know on earth. We will never suffer or be sad again.

But for those left behind on earth, there is sadness. It is hard to say good-bye to someone we love. No matter how many people we love, each one is special. No one else can take that person's place.

When someone we love dies, Jesus understands how we feel and wants to comfort us. He also wants us to continue to show love for people who have died. We can pray for them. We can show respect for their bodies by burying them reverently and by visiting their graves.

Crossword Puzzle

Read the sentences and complete the puzzle with the correct words.

Across

1. When Jesus appeared to the disciples, he said, "_Peace_ be with you."

2. Jesus breathed on his disciples and said, "Receive the Holy _Spirit_."

3. Jesus was sad when his friend _Lazrus_ died.

4. _Mary_ of Magdala was the first one to find the empty tomb.

5. The disciples would spread the _____ _____ that Jesus was risen.

Down

1. The _____ _____ reminds us that Jesus is the light of the world.

Crossword answers filled in grid:
- 1 Across: Peace
- 1 Down: Paschal
- 2 Across: Spirit
- 3 Across: lazarus
- 4 Across: mary
- 5 Across: good news
- Down column: candle

Working for Peace Every Day

Each one of us can work for peace and spread Jesus' message to the world. Fill out the pledge below to share some of the ways you work for peace in your everyday life.

Pledge for Peace

I _Angela Pierre-Louis_ work for peace.
(name)

At school, I work for peace by
Make new awesome friends.

When I play with friends, I work for peace by
playing nicely.

At home, I work for peace by
doing chores

One peaceful thing I want to do better is
help others

115

Complete the Sentences

Write the missing letters on the blanks.

1. By his Resurrection Jesus overcame sin and d e a t h .

2. The feast on which we celebrate Jesus' Resurrection is E a s t e r .

3. If we trust Jesus, he can take away our f e a r s .

4. We celebrate the Resurrection of the Lord each S u n d a y.

5. When we die, Jesus will take us home to h e a v e n .

We Remember

Why do we celebrate Jesus' Resurrection?
We celebrate Jesus' Resurrection because when he destroyed death, he showed he was God. He made it possible for us to live with him forever in heaven.

We Respond

I want to live as a follower of Jesus, our risen Lord. I pray, "Jesus, I trust in your loving care."

Building Family Faith

CHAPTER SUMMARY Jesus rose from the dead. His Resurrection opens the gates of heaven to us. Because Jesus conquered death, we too can look forward to eternal life in heaven.

REFLECT

If, then, we have died with Christ, we believe that we shall also live with him. We know that Christ, raised from the dead, dies no more; death no longer has power over him.

Romans 6:8–9

DISCUSS AS A FAMILY

• Jesus' first words to his disciples after his Resurrection were "Peace be with you." (John 20:21) Where do we need peace in our family?

• Jesus' Resurrection means that he is present in our lives. How is Jesus present to us? Where do we see him in our family?

PRAY

Thank you, Lord Jesus, for giving us new life. Help us see you in all things.

DO

Plan how your family can help bring peace to people in distress. If possible, choose a situation close at hand, such as family members or friends who are ill or suffering.

Visit **www.ChristOurLife.org/family** for more family resources.

Jesus Christ Is Lord and King

Jesus Returned in Glory to His Father

In the Bible, the last time Jesus appeared to his disciples, he gave them this message:

> "Go, therefore, and make disciples of all nations, baptizing them in the name of the Father, and of the Son, and of the holy Spirit, teaching them to observe all that I have commanded you. And behold, I am with you always, until the end of the age."
>
> Matthew 28:19–20

Jesus also told them to return to Jerusalem and wait for the coming of the Holy Spirit. They would receive power from the Holy Spirit and become Christ's **witnesses** before the whole world.

After saying these things Jesus raised his hands in blessing. The disciples saw Jesus being lifted up. Then a cloud covered him, and they could see him no more.

> adapted from the Acts of the Apostles 1:4–8; Luke 24:50

Jesus entered into his Father's presence in heaven. This mystery is called the **Ascension.** The Church celebrates this mystery 40 days after Easter Sunday on Ascension Thursday.

The Paschal Mystery

Jesus saved us through his passion, death, Resurrection, and Ascension into glory. This is called the **Paschal Mystery.** We celebrate the Paschal Mystery at every Mass. We celebrate its saving effects in the sacraments.

May Christ Reign in Our Hearts

Jesus is called Christ the King because he saved us and now sits at the right hand of God the Father. The time of a king's rule is called a **reign.** Christ the King will rule forever. His reign will never end.

Wherever Christ reigns, there is truth, justice, and peace. Every person is respected and treated fairly. People's needs are met. We are all free to use our gifts and to join together in community.

Jesus does not force us to accept him as our king. We can choose to be greedy and selfish. We can choose to say and do things that hurt ourselves and others.

But we will be happy only when we live in love. In Christ's kingdom, love reigns. We let Christ reign in our hearts when we listen to him and obey his teachings.

> Sing praise to God, sing praise;
>   sing praise to our king, sing praise.
> God is king over all the earth;
>   sing hymns of praise.
> God rules over the nations;
>   God sits upon his holy throne.

Psalm 47:7–9

During every Mass, we proclaim Christ as king. After praying the Our Father, we praise God, saying:

For the kingdom, the power and the glory are yours, now and forever.

A Moment with Jesus

Pray the Our Father adding the ending we use at Mass. Think about how awesome God's kingdom is. Thank Jesus for being our good king.

A Crisscross Puzzle

Read the sentences and complete the puzzle with the correct word.

1. Forty days after Easter, Jesus ascended into _____ .

2. Jesus gave a farewell message to his _____ .

3. The Church celebrates Jesus' return to heavenly glory on _____ Thursday.

4. Jesus told his disciples to teach all _____ .

5. Jesus sent his disciples to be his _____ before the whole world.

Crossword puzzle answers:
1. heaven
2. disciples
3. ascension
4. nations
5. witnesses

(down) ASCENSION

Jesus My King

Find the sentences that tell something you can do to show that Jesus is your king. Print the numbers of these sentences in the jewels on the crown. Then print *Christ the King* in the crown.

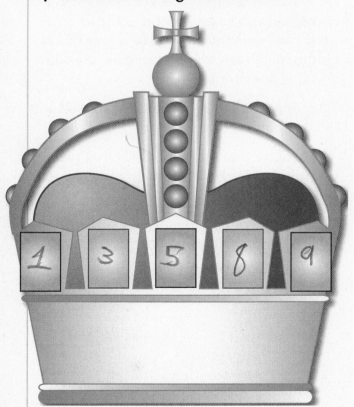

Crown jewels: 1 3 5 8 9

1. Say something friendly to a child who looks lonely or sad.

2. Tease little children.

3. Send a card to someone who is lonely or sick.

4. Complain about food and other things you don't like.

5. Be patient when others do something that upsets you.

6. Argue with your brothers and sisters.

7. Refuse to share new things that you really like.

8. Offer to help others with tasks at home and at school.

9. Pray for other people.

10. Sulk when you don't get what you want.

Jesus Will Come Again

Jesus will come again in glory at the end of time to judge all people. Jesus told his disciples about this judgment. He said, "The Son of Man will come with all his angels and take his seat on his throne. All the people of the earth will be gathered before him. He will separate them into two groups, as a shepherd separates the sheep and the goats."

The king will say to those on his right hand, "Come, you who are blessed by my Father. Receive the kingdom prepared for you from the creation of the world. For I was hungry and you gave me food. I was thirsty and you gave me drink. I was a stranger and you welcomed me. I was naked and you clothed me. I was sick and you visited me, in prison and you came to see me."

Then these people will say, "Lord, when did we see you in want and do these things for you?" The king will answer them, "Whenever you did this to one of the least of mine, you did it to me."

Next he will say to those on his left hand, "Go away from me, to the eternal fire prepared for the devil and his angels. For I was hungry and you gave me no food. I was thirsty and you gave me no drink. I was a stranger and you did not make me welcome, naked and you did not clothe me. I was sick and in prison and you did not care for me."

Then they will ask, "When did we see you in want and not take care of your needs?"

The king will answer them, "What you did not do for one of these least ones, you did not do for me."

They will go away to eternal punishment, and the good will go to eternal life.

adapted from Matthew 25:31–46

How Can We Show Mercy to Others?

Read the sentences. Answer the questions.

1. My little brother is very sad because his goldfish died. What should I do?

    _____

    _____

2. Kayla hasn't been bringing a lunch to school lately. She says she isn't hungry, but I can hear her stomach growling. What should I do?

    _____

    _____

3. Emma likes to make fun of the new boy in school because he has a funny accent. What should I do?

    _____

    _____

4. Anthony broke his leg skateboarding. He is stuck in bed for a while. He is really bored and lonely. What should I do?

    _____

    _____

5. We're learning about fractions in math class. I'm good at adding them together, but my friend Alex is having trouble with them. What should I do?

    _____

    _____

6. Ever since my baby sister was born, Mom and Dad haven't spent as much time with me. I'm feeling really left out. What should I do?

    _____

    _____

7. It's cold outside, but Ethan doesn't have a warm coat. My brother has outgrown his and gotten a new one. The old one is just Ethan's size. What should I do?

    _____

    _____

8. Grandma has to go to the hospital for an operation. My mom is really upset because her mother is so sick. What should I do?

    _____

    _____

We Remember

How do we know that whatever we do for others, we do for Jesus?

Jesus said, "Whatever you do for one of the least of mine, you do for me."

adapted from Matthew 25:40

Words to Know

Ascension **Paschal Mystery**
witness

We Respond

Jesus, I love you.

Blessed Teresa of Calcutta was a witness to Jesus. She showed Jesus' mercy to everyone she met. Her Sisters carry on her work of loving him in the poorest of the poor.

Building Family Faith

CHAPTER SUMMARY The risen Jesus is Lord and King of all creation. One day he will come in glory to judge all people. We honor our king by acting kindly and generously toward others.

REFLECT

Then the king will say to those on his right, "Come, you who are blessed by my Father. Inherit the kingdom prepared for you from the foundation of the world. For I was hungry and you gave me food, I was thirsty and you gave me drink, a stranger and you welcomed me, naked and you clothed me, ill and you cared for me, in prison and you visited me."

Matthew 25:34–36

DISCUSS AS A FAMILY

• Why is it important to reach out to others with love?

• Read the Matthew 25 passage together as a family. Discuss how the loving actions that the king describes take place within your family.

PRAY

Lord Jesus, the kingdom, the power, and the glory are yours, now and forever. Amen.

DO

Ask each family member to describe a need that he or she has. Decide together how you will meet each need.

Visit **www.ChristOurLife.org/family** for more family resources.

Jesus Gives the Spirit to the Church

Jesus Sent the Holy Spirit on Pentecost

Before Jesus died, he made a very special promise to his apostles. He told them:

> "I will send you the Helper, the Holy Spirit, who knows all truth. He comes from the Father and will teach you all about me. Then you can teach other people about me because you have been with me from the beginning."

adapted from John 15:26–27

Jesus kept his promise after he returned to heaven. The apostles waited in Jerusalem as Jesus had told them to do. Mary, the

mother of Jesus, was with them. While they waited for the Holy Spirit, they prayed. Suddenly there was the sound of a loud wind. Something like tongues of fire rested on the heads of those who were there. The Holy Spirit had come! Wind and fire are signs of the Spirit. We celebrate this event on **Pentecost.**

The Holy Spirit Helps God's People

Jesus had sent the Holy Spirit to work in and through the apostles. They were the leaders of his Church. The Holy Spirit helped them grow in love for God and understand what Jesus had taught. He helped them act more like Jesus. The Holy Spirit made it possible for the apostles to carry on what Jesus had done.

- They did the will of God our Father.
- They did works of love.
- They taught all that Jesus had said.
- They prayed as Jesus had taught them.
- They forgave sins.
- They worked and suffered to spread the Kingdom of God.
- They offered Jesus' own sacrifice to the Father.

The Holy Spirit had come with power to help the whole Church do what Jesus had done. The Church is the People of God. We are God's people today. We listen to the Holy Spirit, obey our Church leaders, and do the work of Jesus.

The Holy Spirit Is with Us

The Holy Spirit came at Baptism to live within our hearts. He gives us the grace to love God and others. He helps us understand God's great love for us. The Holy Spirit has special gifts for us. Those gifts help us pray and do the work of Jesus in the world.

The Spirit speaks quietly–often when we are not expecting him. We do not want to miss his voice, so we must always be ready and listening!

Special Messages for You

Put the words below in the correct order. Then you will know how to be ready for the gifts of the Holy Spirit. The first word of each sentence is given.

1. Have _some quiet time to talk to God_ .
   quiet   time   to   God   talk   to   some

2. Pray, "_Come Holy Spirit_ ."
   Spirit   Come   Holy

3. Do _what God asks you_ .
   what   you   asks   God

4. Use _the Holy Spirit's gifts of grace_ .
   grace   the   Spirit's   Holy   of   gifts

5. Thank _the Holy Spirit's for his gifts_ .
   his   Spirit   for   the   Holy   gifts

A Moment with Jesus

Thank Jesus for giving us the gift of the Holy Spirit. Tell Jesus about the ways you listen to the Holy Spirit.

Discover the Special Words

Choose a color for each number and write it in below:

1. _Red_   2. _Blue_   3. _green_

4. _brown_   5. _yellow_   6. _purple_

Use your new color code to decorate the stained glass window. Fill in each numbered space with the color you have chosen for that number. When you have filled in all the spaces, you will see two very special words.

Read the following messages carefully. They also reveal the special words.

First Special Word

The great God who has created all things is our Father! He loves us more than we can imagine. Jesus is happy to share his Father's love with us. He called God "**Abba,** Father." Jewish children used this name, which is like "Dad," for their earthly fathers. Jesus tells us that we too may call God by that name. How wonderful it is that our great, almighty God is our loving heavenly Father!

Second Special Word

Jesus, who loved us so much that he suffered and died for us, is the **Lord!** When Jesus returned to heaven after his Resurrection, God the Father made him Lord of heaven and earth. Jesus, as Lord, wants us to love him and come to him with our joys and sorrows. He wants to be our friend. The Holy Spirit wants us to love Jesus and become like him.

We can use these two special words when we pray to God. The Holy Spirit is with us and gives us the grace to pray and grow in love.

Mary Was Filled with the Spirit

Mary is the best example of what it means to listen to the Holy Spirit. She was full of grace. The Holy Spirit was always with her. However, the Holy Spirit came to Mary in a special way. The Spirit came at the Annunciation when the Father asked her to be the mother of Jesus. Mary also celebrated the presence of the Holy Spirit on Pentecost with the disciples. Think about these events in Mary's life. Ask Mary to help you listen to the Holy Spirit.

Mary, stained glass, Springfield, Illinois

Write about Mary's loving deeds at these special times.

Mary's relative Elizabeth was expecting a baby.

Mary went to
vist

Mary and Jesus were at the wedding at Cana.

He made the water
in to wine.

Jesus was dying on the cross.

She stayed with
her sun a prayed

Kateri Tekakwitha Listened to the Holy Spirit

The Holy Spirit gave Blessed Kateri Tekakwitha three special gifts: love, courage, and desire for prayer. Kateri was grateful for these gifts, and she used them well.

The Holy Spirit gives these gifts to us too. How do you use your gifts of love, courage, and desire for prayer?

Kateri Tekakwitha

Love

I hug my mom everyday

Courage

People were stealing and I walk away

Desire for Prayer

I pray right before I go to bed

We Remember

What does the Holy Spirit do for us?

The Holy Spirit helps us know and love God, pray, and do the work of Jesus.

Words to Know
Abba   Lord   Pentecost

We Respond
Come, Holy Spirit!

Building Family Faith

CHAPTER SUMMARY After he returned to the Father, Jesus sent the Holy Spirit to those who followed him. This same Holy Spirit comes to us at Baptism and enables us to do the work of Christ.

REFLECT

And do not grieve the holy Spirit of God, with which you were sealed for the day of redemption. All bitterness, fury, anger, shouting, and reviling must be removed from you, along with all malice. [And] be kind to one another, compassionate, forgiving one another as God has forgiven you in Christ.

Ephesians 4:30–32

DISCUSS AS A FAMILY

• When did you have a hard time doing the right thing but did it anyway? How were you able to do it?

• At school and at work, how are we challenged to be kind, compassionate, and forgiving?

PRAY

Come, Holy Spirit, and fill the hearts of your faithful, and kindle in them the fire of your love. Send forth your Spirit and they shall be created, and you shall renew the face of the earth.

DO

Pray this Prayer to the Holy Spirit with your child at his or her bedtime.

Visit **www.ChristOurLife.org/family** for more family resources.

We Belong to the Kingdom

Jesus Unites Us in the Communion of Saints

All the people who belong to Christ the King are joined to God and to one another by his love. We call this union the **Communion of Saints.** Everyone in the Communion of Saints works together to praise God and to bring Christ's love to all.

All baptized people belong to the Communion of Saints.

You and I are baptized, so we are members of the Communion of Saints. All your family and friends who are baptized belong to the Communion of Saints.

Write the names of people you love who are members of the Communion of Saints on earth.

_____

_____

_____

All people in purgatory belong to the Communion of Saints.

These are people who died but are not ready to be united with God in heaven.

They believed in Jesus and are saved by him, but the effects of sin still remain. Before they can be completely united with God, they are in **purgatory** getting ready to meet God. They long to be with God in heaven. They know that they will be with God when they are free from sin's effects.

All people in heaven belong to the Communion of Saints.

These are people who died and are ready to be completely united with God. They live with God in heaven. They pray for us and ask God to give us grace and blessings. Their lives can teach us how to become holy. All of us have patron saints in heaven who watch over us with special love. Maybe some of our relatives and friends are now saints in heaven too.

Write the names of some of your favorite saints.

_____

_____

_____

We Are All One in Christ

The members of the Communion of Saints are all one in Christ. Just as in any family, each member helps the other members. The saints in heaven, the souls in purgatory, and the baptized people on earth help us be faithful to God by their prayers. We pray and do good works for all the members of the Communion of Saints on earth. We also help the people in purgatory by our prayers and good works.

The Family of God

Find the word on the gift tag that completes each sentence. Write the words on the lines.

1. People on earth who believe in Jesus and are baptized belong to the Communion of _____ .

2. All in the Communion of Saints are united in Christ's _____ .

3. Those who died and believed in Jesus but were not ready for complete union with God are purified in _____ .

4. We help the people in purgatory by our prayers and good _____ .

5. Members of the Communion of Saints who are perfectly happy are in _____ .

heaven

Saints

purgatory

love

works

Mary Is Queen of Heaven and Earth

At the end of Mary's life on earth, she was taken body and soul into heavenly glory. Mary shared in the Resurrection of Jesus. We call this the **Assumption.** She now rejoices in heaven with the angels and saints. We celebrate the Assumption on August 15.

God made Mary the queen of heaven and earth. God wants Mary to take care of us. She helps us follow Jesus. This is why we pray to her. Someday when we die, we will also share in the Resurrection of Jesus. In heaven our bodies will be glorified like the risen Jesus' body. We will be united with Jesus, Mary, the angels, the saints, and all those we love in heaven.

What prayer can we pray to Mary to ask her to help us love God?

After Mary's Assumption, God crowned her as Queen of Heaven.

Hail, Holy Queen, Enthroned Above

1. Hail, holy Queen, enthroned above,
   O Maria.
   Hail, Mother of mercy and of love,
   O Maria.
   Triumph, all ye cherubim,
   Sing with us, ye seraphim,
   Heav'n and earth resound the hymn:
   Salve, Salve, Salve Regina.

2. The cause of joy to all below,
   O Maria.
   The spring through which all graces flow,
   O Maria.
   Angels all your praises bring,
   Earth and heaven with us sing,
   All creation echoing:
   Salve, Salve, Salve Regina.

We Honor Mary

The Church honors Mary because she is the mother of Jesus. When we honor Mary, we praise God because God gave her the gifts of holiness and faithfulness.

In the Litany of Our Lady, we honor Mary with many titles. As we say each title, we think of a special gift God gave her. After we say each title, we ask Mary to pray for us. She will ask Jesus for the grace we need to be holy.

Mary is featured on a bronze holy medal above. Our Lady of Guadalupe, below, is a detail from a mosaic in the Church of the Dormition, Jerusalem, Israel.

From the Litany of Our Lady

Response: Pray for us.

Holy Mary,
Holy Mother of God,
Mother of Christ,
Mother most pure,
Virgin most merciful,
Virgin most faithful,
Help of Christians,
Queen of apostles,
Queen of martyrs,
Queen of all saints,
Queen of the most holy rosary,
Queen of peace.

Let us pray: Pray for us, O holy mother of God.

Response: That we may be made worthy of the promises of Christ. Amen.

Our Lady of Guadalupe

Our Lady of Guadalupe is one of the titles we give to Mary. In 1531 Mary appeared to an Aztec man named Juan Diego. She was dressed as an Aztec woman to show her love and compassion to an oppressed group of people. Mary had heard the prayers and pain of these people. She came to give them hope. Our Lady of Guadalupe is honored because of her motherly concern for people in need.

Acting like a Member of the Communion of Saints

Write under each picture what you can do to be a faithful person like Mary.

We Belong to God's Kingdom

Print the correct letters on the lines.

1. Jesus is truly the S __ __ of God.

2. Jesus r __ __ __ from the dead.

3. Jesus returned to his Father in
   g __ __ __ __ .

4. Our bodies will r __ __ __ on
   the last day as Jesus promised.

5. All those who die to s __ __ will
   share in the glory of the risen Jesus.

6. The s __ __ __ __ __ in
   heaven pray to God for us.

7. The Holy S __ __ __ __ __
   gives us grace to be strong Christians.

Illustration of the Communion of Saints by Elizabeth Wang, "The Glory and the Gathering," © Radiant Light 2006, www.radiantlight.org.uk

We Remember

What is the Communion of Saints?
The Communion of Saints is the union of all those who belong to Christ the King. It includes all the saints in heaven, all the souls in purgatory, and all the baptized people on earth.

Why do we honor Mary?
We honor Mary because she is the mother of Jesus. We praise God for her many gifts.

Words to Know
Assumption   Communion of Saints
purgatory

We Respond

Holy Mary, Mother of God,
pray for us sinners,
now and at the hour
of our death.

Which Words?

Underline the best choice to complete each sentence.

1. Jesus said he came into the world to (save, blame, battle) the world.

2. Jesus said that we do for him what we (do in church, say in our prayers, do for others).

3. Jesus said his followers must (carry their cross, work for more money, seek a good job).

4. People who have died but are not yet ready to meet God are in (heaven, purgatory, hell).

5. The sacrifice of the New Covenant is the (Sacrament of Reconciliation, Mass celebration, Passover celebration).

6. The Holy Spirit came to (guide, judge, control).

7. Jesus will share his glory with those who are (smart, loving, rich).

Christ the King

Fill in the missing letters. Use the words in the crown.

Jesus is our K __ __ __.

He __ __ i __ __ __ in heaven and on earth.

Jesus promised __ __ __ __ __ n __ __ __ to us.

He invites us to share his g __ __ __ __.

Jesus will come to __ __ d __ __ all people at the end of time.

He will be __ o __ __ forever and ever.

We are already one with him in __ __ m __ __ __ __ __ __.

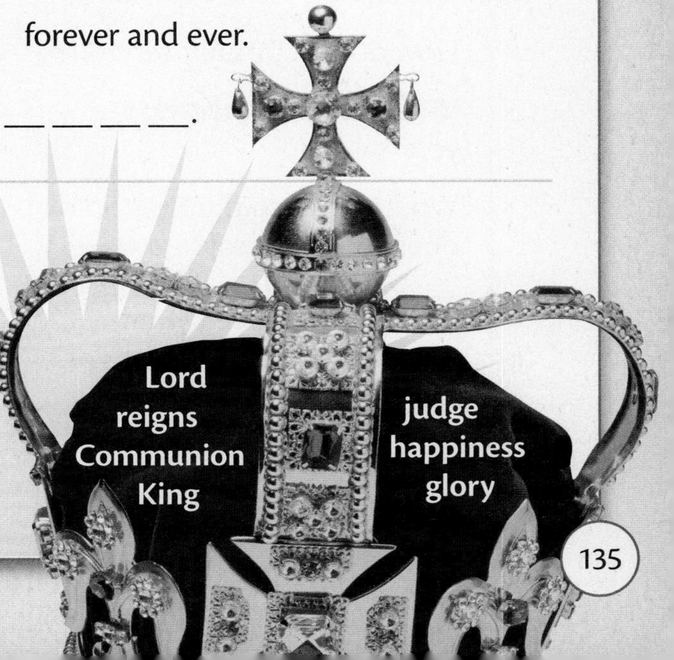

Lord
reigns
Communion
King

judge
happiness
glory

Paschal Mystery Crisscross Puzzle

Write the missing letters of the four main events of Jesus' life:

```
P _ _ _ _ _
A
S                    M
C                    Y
H          _ _   S _ _ _ _ _ _ _ _ _
_ _ A _ _          T
   L          _ _ _ E _ _ _ _ _
             R
             Y
```

Draw a Picture of a Saint

Have you noticed how a picture of a saint tells a story about that saint? Draw a saint for this window and tell us a story by adding details of clothing and symbols.

- What kind of clothes does your saint wear?

- What symbols belong to your saint?

Think about the life of your saint.

- How does your saint serve God?

- What works of mercy does your saint do?

- What prayer to the Holy Spirit does your saint say?

When you have finished your picture story, write your saint's name at the bottom. Don't forget to draw a halo!

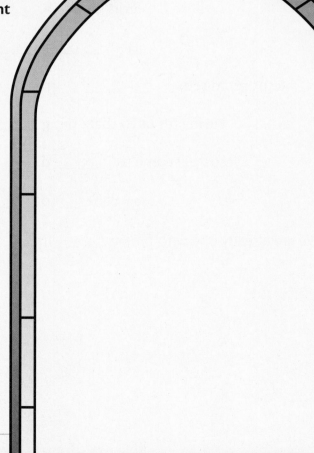

Come Lord Jesus

Reader 1: We are never alone on our journey of faith to heaven. We are part of a great family of saints. The whole family of God in heaven, in purgatory, and on earth is united in God's life and his love. This union of God's children, the Communion of Saints, will last forever in heaven.

Reader 2: We are waiting for the coming of Jesus and the kingdom of heaven. We wait in joy, looking forward to all the wonderful things God has promised to those who are faithful. While we wait, we pray, love, and serve. We try to do all the good we can. We try to spread God's kingdom— to bring his truth and love to others. This is how Jesus wants us to wait for his coming.

Reader 3: See that you are prepared; have your lamps lit. Be like servants waiting for their master to return, ready to open the door as soon as he comes and knocks. How happy will those servants be whom the master finds ready when he comes!

adapted from Luke 12:35–37

Leader: We will light candles as a sign that we want to be ready when God calls us to heaven.

(Light candles.)

Reader 4: The burning lamp is a symbol of our faith. We keep our lamps burning by living in faith, hope, and love until Jesus comes to call us home forever. Saint John wrote in the last book of the Bible about waiting for the Lord's return. Jesus revealed this message to John for his Church.

Reader 5: I am coming soon! Let those who do good keep on doing good. Those who are holy must keep on being holy. I am coming soon! I will bring with me the reward for everyone according to what he or she deserves. Yes, I am coming soon!

adapted from
Revelation 22:11–12,20

Reader 6: In response to this message, Saint John wrote the closing words of Sacred Scripture:

All: Amen! Come, Lord Jesus!

(Put out candles.)

Leader: Let us pray to our patron saints. Each of us may name his or her own saint, and all of us will answer, "Pray for us." We may also include names of people we have known who are now in eternity.

All: Dear saints of God, you followed Jesus faithfully on earth and now enjoy the reward Jesus promised. Pray for us who still struggle against sin. Obtain for us the help we need to serve God faithfully. May we one day be with you in the heavenly kingdom. Amen.

Family Feature

Roots and Branches:

Family Stories and Family Faith

The Catholic faith that we pass on to our children is an important part of our heritage. We adults possess this faith because other people passed it on to us. The line of our ancestors in faith stretches thousands of years into the past. But, for almost all of us, this heritage of faith is also very present and alive in the stories of our family. One of the best ways to build faith in our children is to share our stories with them. Family history includes memories of those who are no longer with us and the living stories of the aunts and uncles, grandparents and cousins, nieces and nephews in your child's extended family. In the history of your family, your child will learn some of the most important lessons of faith.

Family Feature

Strengthening Your Child's Connection to Your Family's History

Reach out to your extended family.

Time pressures and distance can make keeping up with the people in your extended family difficult, but it's worth the effort to make sure your child gets to know his or her grandparents, aunts, uncles, and cousins. Your own extended family might also include godparents and other close family friends, even though they may not be related by blood. This loving group can be an invaluable resource for children as they awaken to the larger world. In the wisdom and experience of family, children can find answers to the big questions of life: "Is the world a friendly or a scary place?" "What do I stand for?" "What do we believe in?"

Connect across the generations.

Encourage your children to speak with grandparents, aunts, uncles, and other older relatives about what their faith means to them. An open-ended approach usually works best. Your child might ask them what they remember about their First Communion or Confirmation. Did they ever think about becoming a nun or a priest? Do they have a favorite saint? If they were born in another country or grew up with parents who were, what do they remember of special religious customs of their childhood?

Tell the milestone stories.

Talk about the day your child was born. What were you doing when the excitement started? (Children usually love to hear about the rush to the hospital.) What did Grandpa and Grandma say when you called with the news of their birth? Talk about the day of your child's Baptism. How did you choose your child's name? What's the significance of this name? Was he or she named for another family member or a dear family friend?

When I was a child . . .

Children like to hear their elders talk about the time when they were young (as long as the stories are honest and funny, and not occasions for preaching). They like knowing that their parents and aunts and uncles faced the same insecurities and indignities they face. These stories help them absorb a useful perspective on life: their parents were once young. They themselves will grow up and assume adult responsibilities like the older people in their family.

Borrow strength from your relatives.

It's likely that your relatives and ancestors faced challenges very similar to the ones your family faces. They struggled to make a living, raise children, and make a home. They coped with illness and death, unwelcome relocation, separation from loved ones, and financial setbacks. Their faith sustained them. Probe for the stories of this practical faith and share them with your children. Climb the family tree. At the top, you'll get the best view of life.

Visit **www.ChristOurLife.org/family** for more family resources.

Don't hide the negative in your family history.

Every family's story has its bleak chapters. Talk about them in a straightforward way when your child is ready to hear about them. God does not want us to hide or deny problems and difficulties, but to embrace them with faith and courage.

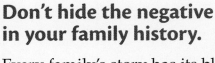

Family Feature

The Story of a Family Challenge

Ask your child to solicit a "Favorite Family Story" from a relative. It should be the story of a challenging situation that shows the power of faith. You might suggest a grandparent or aunt or uncle who is close to your child and who has a lively appreciation for the family's story. Have your child sit down and fill out the story sheet below. Then ask your child to make a cover for the story "book" with a drawing that illustrates the story.

My Favorite Family Story

Who told the story? _____

_____

The Story: _____

_____

_____

_____

_____

_____

_____

What was the challenge? _____

_____

_____

How did God help? _____

_____

_____

Jesus Is with Us on Our Way

"Go, therefore, and make disciples of all nations, baptizing them in the name of the Father, and of the Son, and of the holy Spirit, teaching them to observe all that I have commanded you. And behold, I am with you always, until the end of the age."

Matthew 28:19–20

A Letter Home

Dear Parents and Family,

The sacraments are a great gift from God. They help us answer our call to be holy, and they provide a tangible experience of God's grace, forgiveness, and love. Unit 5 explores three of the sacraments.

Chapter 20 tells how Baptism offers us the chance to live a life of grace. The children will discover that through Baptism, God dwells within us and allows us to live as his children.

In the sacraments, we experience the Holy Spirit, who brings us spiritual gifts and guides us in how to live as God's children. In Chapter 21, the children will learn that the Holy Spirit helps us reflect the Lord's image, each according to our own gifts.

Jesus' forgiveness is the joyful message of Chapter 22. The children will learn that Jesus is always ready to forgive our sins just as he forgave Saint Peter and others. Jesus calls us to repent and to reconcile ourselves with him, with the Father, and with one another. We need only to trust in him and allow his love to change our lives.

The Sacrament of Penance and Reconciliation is a concrete experience of that love and forgiveness. Though we reject God when we sin, he always welcomes us when we turn to him. The children will review what they have learned about the Sacrament of Reconciliation, and they will learn how to carefully prepare for and reverently celebrate the sacrament.

In Unit 5, the children also will learn of God's invitation to come together as a family to the eucharistic celebration. The children will learn how we take the gifts of the earth, which God has given, and through our human effort create bread and wine. At the Eucharist, the bread and wine are changed into the Body and Blood of Jesus, whose sacrifice is a gift to us. We can make our lives gifts to our heavenly Father in return.

By sharing in the Eucharist, we as God's children can become more like Jesus, sharing his peace and love with others. As we open our home and our hearts to friends, family, neighbors, or even strangers, we recreate this gift of peace and love ourselves.

At the end of each chapter, the children will bring home a family reflection and activity based on the chapter to help nurture the family's faith at home.

Visit **www.ChristOurLife.org/family** for more family resources.

God Shares the Wondrous Life of Grace

Jesus Brings Us a Share in God's Life

God loved the first people he made very much. He wanted them to enjoy a close friendship with him. So God shared his own life, or grace, with them. He made them in his image so that they belonged to his family. They could live forever.

But Adam and Eve had the power to choose. They turned away God's friendship. They chose to disobey God and sinned. They lost grace and were expelled from paradise.

Adam and Eve's sin brought something new into the world. Because of this first sin, people now are born without grace. We tend to be selfish and not love God. This is what it means to be born in original sin.

Adam and Eve were sorry for what they had done. God's love for us was so great that he sent his own Son, Jesus, to save us from sin and death. Because Jesus died and rose for us, we can share in God's life again. We can belong to God's family as his children. We can live with God forever in heaven.

Underline the word or phrase that completes each sentence.

1. God gave his life to Adam and Eve so that they would (be his children, be as great as he is, not obey him).

2. Our share in God's life is called (love, grace, hope).

3. God sent (Adam and Eve, Mary, Jesus) to save us from sin and death.

4. We are born in original sin, which means without (sight, speech, the life of grace).

We Receive the Life of Grace in Baptism

An important man named Nicodemus came to Jesus. He said to Jesus, "We know that you are a teacher from God. No one else can do the things you do. God is with you."

Jesus told him, "You must be born of water and the Spirit to enter God's kingdom."

"How can that be?" Nicodemus asked.

Jesus was talking about Baptism. Through his death on the cross and his rising, Jesus gives God's life in Baptism to those who believe in him.

Jesus reminded Nicodemus of how much God loves the world.

> God so loved the world that he gave his only Son, so that everyone who believes in him may have eternal life.
>
> adapted from John 3:16

Jesus told Nicodemus that God sent the Son to save people, not to condemn them. He wants everyone to belong to God's kingdom.

Baptism Is a Sacrament

We celebrate the gift of new life in God in the Sacrament of Baptism. Most of us were baptized as infants. Our parents and godparents took us to church. They promised to help us live as Christians.

Then the priest or deacon baptized us with water. He called us by name and said, "I baptize you in the name of the Father, and of the Son, and of the Holy Spirit."

These words and the water are the signs in the Sacrament of Baptism. When they are used, we are given new life in Jesus.

God gives us grace, takes away original sin, and forgives our sins. In Baptism we tell God that we want to keep away from sin and follow his Son. We become God's children and are welcomed into God's family, the Church.

We Are Headed for Heaven

Throughout our life, we long to be with God in heaven. The sacraments help us on our way to heaven. When we are in heaven, we will fully share in God's life. As we know from the Apostle's Creed, we will share in "the resurrection of the body, and the life everlasting."

So what is heaven like? Think of a time when you were your most happy and surrounded by beauty and joy. Take that feeling and multiply it by 100. Heaven is even more beautiful and joyous than that! In the Bible, Paul describes heaven this way:

> No one has ever seen or heard anything like it! No one can imagine what wonderful things God has prepared for those who love him.
>
> adapted from 1 Corinthians 2:9

The Life Everlasting

Draw or write the names of some people and things you hope to find in heaven:

Living the Life of Grace

At Baptism we received the grace to live a new life in Jesus. We can grow more like him. In addition to the sacraments, there are many things we can do to live more like Jesus.

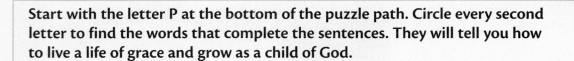

Start with the letter P at the bottom of the puzzle path. Circle every second letter to find the words that complete the sentences. They will tell you how to live a life of grace and grow as a child of God.

1. _____ every day.

2. Listen when the _____ is read. Try to read from it yourself.

3. Receive Jesus in Holy _____ .

4. Obey God's _____ .

5. _____ the gifts God has given you.

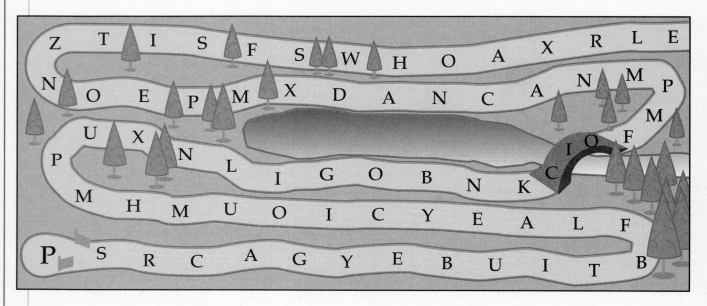

Z T I S F S W H O A X R L E
N O E P M X D A N C A N M P
U X N M
P L I G O B N K C I O F M
M H M U O I C Y E A L F
P S R C A G Y E B U I T B

A Moment with Jesus

Talk to Jesus using the words of the psalm.

You will show me the path to life.
With you, there is boundless joy.
In your right hand there is happiness forever.

adapted from Psalm 16:11

A Puzzle About Baptism

Fill in the missing words in the acrostic puzzle. The sentences and the Word Bank will help you.

WORD BANK

water   family   life
grace   Jesus

1. In Baptism we share in God's life called
   _____ .

2. _____ is poured on us
   when we are baptized.

3. The grace we receive in Baptism is new
   _____ .

4. _____ told us that we
   can live with him if we are baptized.

5. Through Baptism we become
   members of the Church, God's
   _____ .

God Shares His Life

All the sacraments are special ways in which God shares his life with us. Match the name of a sacrament (Baptism, Reconciliation, Eucharist) with each picture here.

_____   _____   _____

Celebrating Baptism

Do you know someone who was baptized recently? Create a greeting card below to welcome him or her into God's family.

We Remember

What does Baptism do for us?
Baptism gives us new life in Jesus. We become members of the Church and children of God.

We Respond

You will show me the path to life, joy, and happiness forever.

adapted from Psalm 16:11

Building Family Faith

CHAPTER SUMMARY In Baptism we receive new life in Christ and the gift of the Holy Spirit. We grow in grace through prayer, Mass, the sacraments, and by sharing Christ's love with others.

REFLECT
Peter [said] to them, "Repent and be baptized, every one of you, in the name of Jesus Christ for the forgiveness of your sins; and you will receive the gift of the holy Spirit."

Acts of the Apostles 2:38

DISCUSS AS A FAMILY
• Share stories of Baptism. Describe the day of your child's Baptism. If you have witnessed adult Baptisms at the Easter Vigil, describe them.
• Baptism brings us into a new family, the Church. How is the Church family like our family?

PRAY
You visit the earth and water it,
make it abundantly fertile.
God's stream is filled with water

Psalm 65:10

DO
Plan a small family party on or near the anniversary of your child's Baptism. Share family photos of the event. Serve your child's favorite treats.

Visit **www.ChristOurLife.org/family** for more family resources.

CHAPTER 21

The Holy Spirit Lives Within Us

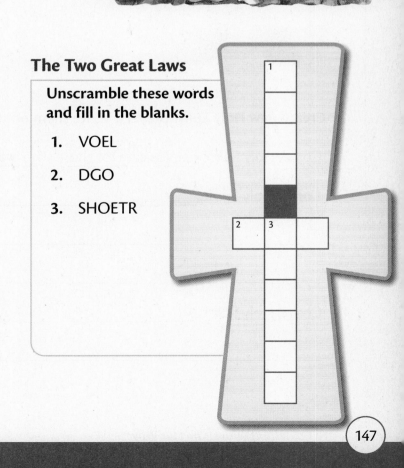

Jesus Is the Way to Eternal Life

Once a rich young man asked Jesus, "What must I do to have eternal life?"

Jesus said, "Keep the commandments."

The man told Jesus, "I have kept all these since I was a boy."

Then Jesus answered, "If you want to show your love, go and sell all you have. Give the money to the poor. Then come and follow me. You will have treasure in heaven."

adapted from Mark 10:17–21

Jesus taught the man that he had to let go of his earthly treasure to gain a more valuable treasure in heaven. What is the heavenly treasure?

_____

Jesus knew that being with God forever was worth giving up everything. No riches on earth are as wonderful as a true friendship with God.

The Two Great Laws

Unscramble these words and fill in the blanks.

1. VOEL

2. DGO

3. SHOETR

The Holy Spirit Is Our Helper

The rich young man had a hard time giving up everything. Sometimes it is hard to follow Jesus. So Jesus sent us a helper.

The Holy Spirit helps us live as God's children. The Spirit helps us follow Jesus.

We celebrate the presence of the Holy Spirit in us in Baptism. He is always with us.

A Moment with Jesus

Thank Jesus for giving us the Spirit. Pray the Holy Spirit prayer.

Come, Holy Spirit, fill the hearts of your faithful, And kindle in them the fire of your love.

Create new Holy Spirit prayers. Write them on the lines below. One is done for you.

Come, Holy Spirit, <u>help us care for those who are sick and comfort those who are sad.</u>

Come, Holy Spirit, _____

_____

_____

Come, Holy Spirit, _____

_____

The Holy Spirit Leads Us to Do Good

The Spirit makes us more like Jesus. Saint Paul tells us:

> Like mirrors we reflect the brightness of the Lord. We grow brighter and brighter as we are changed into the image of Jesus. This is the work of the Holy Spirit.

> adapted from 2 Corinthians 3:18

The Holy Spirit shares his own goodness with us and leads us to heaven.

The words around the dove tell us some of the good things the Holy Spirit shares.

Patience
Kindness
Love
Faith
Joy
Peace
Generosity

The Holy Spirit Helps Us Avoid Evil

With the Spirit's help we can overcome temptations and avoid sin. A temptation is something that makes us want to do what is wrong. A **personal sin** is when we choose to do wrong. We sin when we think, say, or do what we know offends God. When we sin, we may also hurt ourselves and others. Saint Paul tells us that the Holy Spirit helps us do good and avoid evil. He says:

> If you let the Holy Spirit lead you, you will not be selfish.

> People who are selfish make enemies. They fight and argue. They hurt themselves and others.

If the Spirit leads you, you will be full of love, joy, peace, kindness, and goodness.

Since the Spirit has given us life, let us also follow the Spirit.

adapted from Galatians 5:16,19,25

The Holy Spirit helps us be truly wise. If we listen to the Holy Spirit, we will know what is good and what is evil. We will be able to say no to temptation and sin. We will be able to do what is good.

The Holy Spirit gives us special help when we pray and celebrate the sacraments.

Color all the roads the Spirit would tell you to take from Old Town to New Town.

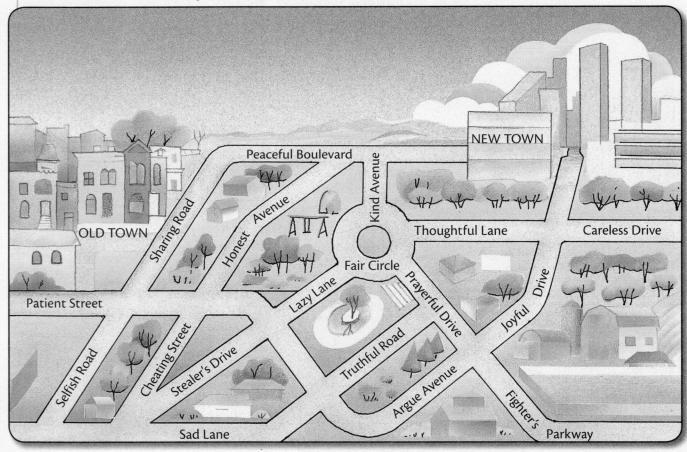

The Holy Spirit Is Our Friend

Complete the sentence beneath each picture. Use the words in the Word Bank.

WORD BANK

Reconciliation
pray
Communion

The Holy Spirit guides us and helps us know what is good when we

_____ .

The Holy Spirit fills us with grace when we are at Mass and receive Holy

_____ .

The Holy Spirit helps us say no to sin when we celebrate the Sacrament of

_____ .

A Story About the Holy Spirit and Me

Write a story about how the Holy Spirit brings good things into your life.

My Story

_____

_____

_____

_____

_____

_____

Saint Dominic Savio

Dominic Savio was a young boy who always tried to listen to the Holy Spirit. Like other children, he faced many temptations. With the help of the Holy Spirit, he was able to choose to do what was right. He once said: "I can't do big things, but I want all that I do to be for the glory of God." He shows us that even small things are holy when they are done for God.

We Remember

How does the Holy Spirit help us?
The Holy Spirit helps us to be more like Jesus, do good, and avoid sin.

What is sin?
Sin is choosing to think, say, or do what we know offends God and what may also hurt ourselves and others.

Words to Know
personal sin

We Respond

Come, Holy Spirit, fill the hearts of your faithful, and kindle in them the fire of your love.

Building Family Faith

CHAPTER SUMMARY Jesus sent the Holy Spirit to help us. The Spirit comes to us at Baptism and is present in us throughout our lives, showing us how to become more like Jesus.

REFLECT

Then there appeared to them tongues as of fire, which parted and came to rest on each one of them. And they were all filled with the holy Spirit.
Acts of the Apostles 2:3–4

DISCUSS AS A FAMILY

• The Holy Spirit is a helper. When did we feel that we needed help today?

• Describe a time when you asked God for help and received it. How did it feel to ask for help?

• How can we help one another in our family?

PRAY

Come, Holy Spirit, fill the hearts of your faithful, and kindle in them the fire of your love.

DO

At bedtime, pray a prayer to the Holy Spirit. Suggest that your child ask the Holy Spirit's help for a particular need.

Visit **www.ChristOurLife.org/family** for more family resources.

God Blesses Contrite Hearts

Jesus Forgave Peter

At the Last Supper Jesus said to Peter, "Simon, the devil will tempt you, but I have prayed that your faith will not fail." Peter loved Jesus and promised, "Lord, I will go to prison and die with you."

Jesus knew that Peter was weak. He warned, "Before the rooster crows today, you will deny three times that you know me."

After the supper Jesus and the apostles went to a garden. There Jesus said, "Pray that you will not be tempted." Then he went to pray to his Father. When he came back, the apostles were asleep. "Why are you sleeping?" Jesus asked. "Get up and pray."

As Jesus spoke, a crowd came to arrest him. They took him away to judge him. Peter followed.

A girl saw Peter and said, "This man also was with Jesus." Peter said, "I do not know him."

After a while a man noticed Peter and said, "You are one of his friends." But Peter answered, "My friend, I am not!"

Later another man said of Peter, "Surely this man was with Jesus. He is a Galilean." Peter said, "I do not know what you are talking about."

While he was saying this, the rooster crowed. Just then, Jesus turned and looked at Peter. Peter remembered the Lord's words and went out and wept.

Jesus, who loved Peter, knew his sorrow and forgave him. He made Peter the head of his Church.

adapted from Luke 22:31–62

Forgiveness of Sins

Just as Peter said and did things that set him apart from Jesus, we also say and do things that set us apart from God. Sin is anything that separates us from God and from other people. Just as Jesus forgave Peter, God calls us to be sorry so we can receive his forgiveness.

Jesus Forgives Those Who Are Sorry

Do you remember these Bible stories? What do they teach us about God and sinners?

The Two Men in the Temple

Two men went up to the Temple to pray. The first man thought of the good things he had done and prayed: "O God, I thank you that I am not like other people—greedy, dishonest, and unkind. I thank you that I am better than this tax collector."

The other man stayed far back and bowed his head. He thought of the times he had not kept all of God's commandments. He said, "O God, be merciful to me, a sinner." God was pleased with the second man because he was sorry. This man went home with God's peace, but the other did not.

adapted from Luke 18:10–14

Jesus and the Woman at Simon's House

One day a man named Simon invited Jesus to his house for a meal. While Jesus and the other guests were eating, a woman came into the room. She was sad because she had not always kept God's laws of love. She came to tell Jesus she was sorry.

The woman went straight to Jesus. She washed his feet with her tears. She wiped them with her long hair and anointed them with perfumed oil. Jesus looked at her with love. He was pleased that she was sorry.

Simon did not like this. He thought Jesus should not let a sinner touch him. Jesus knew what Simon was thinking and said, "This woman's many sins have been forgiven, so she has shown great love."

Then Jesus spoke to the woman and said: "Your sins are forgiven. Go in peace." The woman's heart was filled with peace and joy.

adapted from Luke 7:36–50

The Shepherd and His Lost Sheep

A man had 100 sheep. One ran away and got lost. The shepherd loved the lost sheep, just as he loved all the sheep in his flock. Because he knew the others were all right, he left them and went to look for the lost one. He searched everywhere until he found it. Then he lifted it up on his shoulders and with great joy carried it back.

When he got home, he invited his friends and neighbors to celebrate. He said, "Rejoice with me because I have found my lost sheep." In the same way, there is great joy in heaven whenever a sinner is sorry.

adapted from Luke 15:4–7

Jesus and Zacchaeus

One day Jesus was passing through the town of Jericho. A rich tax collector named Zacchaeus, who was very short, climbed a tree to see Jesus. When Jesus saw him, he said, "Zacchaeus, come down quickly, for I must stay at your house today."

Zacchaeus hurried down and welcomed Jesus with joy. Some people began to grumble, "Jesus has gone to the house of a sinner."

But Zacchaeus was sorry for cheating the people. He told Jesus and the people, "I will give half of my belongings to the poor. If I have cheated anyone, I will pay back four times as much."

Jesus was pleased and said, "The blessing of God has come to this house today."

adapted from Luke 19:1–10

Do We Have a Disciple's Heart?

The Holy Spirit helps each of us examine our **conscience** to see how we have kept God's laws. When we admit and are sorry for our sins, God gives us peace. A daily **examination of conscience** helps us see where we have strayed from God. Then we can remove those things that offend God from our hearts. We become more loving disciples of Jesus.

Examination of Conscience

1. Have I prayed attentively to God each morning and evening?

2. Have I always used God's name with love and respect?

3. Have I celebrated Sundays and holy days with Mass? How well have I participated?

4. Have I obeyed my parents and others in authority? How have I shown them love and respect?

5. How have I cared for the gift of life—my health and that of others? Do I show respect for my body and the bodies of others?

6. Have I used my gifts to serve God and others? How kind have I been to my family? to other children? to people who are in need?

7. How well have I cared for the gifts of God? Have I shared with those in need?

8. Have I spoken the truth? kept secrets and promises? been kind? spoken up for what is right?

Act of Contrition

My God,
I am sorry for my sins with all my heart.
In choosing to do wrong
and failing to do good,
I have sinned against you
whom I should love above all things.
I firmly intend, with your help,
to do penance,
to sin no more,
and to avoid whatever leads me to sin.
Our Savior Jesus Christ
suffered and died for us.
In his name, my God, have mercy.

A Moment with Jesus

Share with Jesus things for which you are sorry. Read the kind and forgiving words of Jesus.

"You are forgiven. Go in peace."

adapted from Luke 7:48,50

Help the Flowers Grow

An examination of conscience is a little like weeding a garden. You pull out the weeds of temptation and sin to make room for the flowers of love and faith. Can you find any "weeds" in this garden? Circle them to pull them out.

22 Review

Complete the Quotation

WORD BANK

forgiven   rejoice   sinner
blessing   tempted

Complete the sentences. Use the words in the Word Bank.

1. The man in the temple said, "O God be merciful to me, a

   _____ ."

2. Jesus told the woman at Simon's house, "Your sins are

   _____ . Go in peace."

3. To Peter, Jesus said, "Pray that you

   will not be _____ ."

4. When the shepherd found his lost sheep, he called his friends and said

   "_____ with me because I have found my lost sheep."

5. When Zacchaeus said he was sorry that he had cheated people, Jesus

   said, "The _____ of God has come to this house today."

We Remember

When does God forgive us?
God forgives us when we respond to his grace and are sorry for our sins.

Word to Know
conscience
examination of conscience

We Respond
I am sorry for my sins with all my heart.

Building Family Faith

CHAPTER SUMMARY Sin separates us from God and from other people, but God is always ready to forgive us and to restore us to his friendship.

REFLECT
Peter [said] to them, "Repent and be baptized, every one of you, in the name of Jesus Christ for the forgiveness of your sins; and you will receive the gift of the holy Spirit."
                                    Acts of the Apostles 2:38

DISCUSS AS A FAMILY
• As a family, read the four Gospel stories about forgiveness found on pages 154–155 of the student book. Which is your favorite, and why?

• In the story of the woman at Simon's house, Jesus taught that the more we are forgiven, the more we love. What did he mean by this?

PRAY
My God, I am sorry for all my sins with all my heart.

DO
Encourage your child to make an examination of conscience (see page 156).

Visit **www.ChristOurLife.org/family** for more family resources.

CHAPTER 23

God Forgives Us

A Father Forgives His Son

Jesus told this story about a father and son.

Narrator: Once there was a rich man who had two sons. One day the younger son came to his father and said,

Son: Father, give me my share of the money. I am tired of living at home. I want to see some new things.

Father: I am sorry that you want to leave home, but here is the money.

Narrator: The son was happy at first. He wasted his money having a good time with his friends. When the money ran out, his friends left him. He had to find work because he had nothing to eat. The only job he could get was feeding pigs. Even then he was hungry most of the time. One day he sat down to think about what he had done.

Son: What have I done? I have hurt my father. I have hurt myself. Even the pigs have more food than I do.

Narrator: Then the son began to feel sorry for the way he had behaved.

Son: I am so sorry that I hurt my father. He worked so hard for that money.

continued on page 160

Narrator: The young man tried to decide what he should do about it.

Son: I know what I will do. I will go back to my father. I will never be so selfish again. I will try to please my father.

Narrator: The son tried to think of what to say to his father.

Son: I will tell my father what I have done and that I am sorry.

Narrator: The young man wanted to do something to make up to his father for what he had done.

Son: I will do anything he wants. I will work as a servant in his house.

Narrator: The son went home. When he was still a long way off, his father saw him coming. He ran to meet his son. The father put his arms around him and welcomed him.

Son: Father, I am sorry.

Father: Welcome home, my son. You are forgiven. Servants, bring him the finest robe, a ring, and sandals. Come, we must celebrate!

adapted from Luke 15:11–24

A Moment with Jesus

Imagine the son standing before his forgiving father. Now imagine that you are standing before Jesus. What do you say to Jesus?

The Sacrament of Penance and Reconciliation

God loves us, even when we fail to love him and others. Like the son in the story, we ask the forgiveness of our Father in heaven. God calls us to be sorry so we can be ready to receive his forgiveness. God wants to be reconciled with us. He gives us the strength to make up for what we have done. We celebrate God's forgiveness in the Sacrament of Reconciliation.

Draw a picture of yourself telling God that you are sorry.

We Prepare for the Sacrament of Reconciliation

Here are some things I can do to prepare to receive the Sacrament of Reconciliation.

1. Ask the Holy Spirit for help.
2. Examine my conscience.
3. Pray the Act of Contrition.
4. Promise to do better.
5. Ask God to help me love him and others more.

Ten Steps to Confession

When I celebrate the Sacrament of Penance and Reconciliation, I meet Jesus. I meet him in my heart and through the priest who hears my confession.

1. The priest welcomes me. I greet him.

2. I make the Sign of the Cross and say how long it has been since my last confession.

3. I listen to the priest's prayer and Scripture reading.

4. I confess my sins. I may tell the priest any problems I face in living as a Catholic, and I may ask questions.

5. I listen to the priest. Then he gives me a penance.

6. I pray the Act of Contrition.

7. When the priest gives me absolution, I make the Sign of the Cross.

8. The priest may say, "Give thanks to the Lord, for he is good." I answer, "His mercy endures forever."

9. The priest may say something like "Good-bye. God loves you." I say, "Thank you, Father," and I leave.

10. I thank God for his forgiving love and peace. I ask the Holy Spirit to help me live as God's loving child. I do the penance the priest has given me. If it is a prayer, I pray it right away. If it is a deed, I do it as soon as I can.

6. Live as God's _____ .

5. Do your _____ .

4. _____ your sins.

Climb the Peace Tree

Fill in the missing words. Use the words in the Word Bank.

WORD BANK

promise   penance
sorry   confess
examine   loving child

3. _____ to do better.

2. Be _____ .

1. _____ your conscience.

23 Review

Jesus Forgives Us

Print the missing words in the squares to finish the Peace Flag. Use the Word Bank.

P Jesus gave the apostles and _____ power to forgive sins.

E When we tell our sins to the priest, we _____ them.

A When we carefully look over what we have done, we _____ our conscience.

C Jesus loves _____ hearts.

E The priest gives us a _____ to make up for our sins and to turn us away from them.

We Remember

What does Jesus do for us in the Sacrament of Penance and Reconciliation?

Jesus forgives us and gives us his peace and love in the Sacrament of Penance and Reconciliation.

We Respond

Give thanks to the LORD, who is good, whose love endures forever.

Psalm 118:1

Building Family Faith

CHAPTER SUMMARY Jesus restores us to friendship with God in the Sacrament of Penance and Reconciliation. In this sacrament, we express our sorrow for sin and receive forgiveness.

REFLECT

"But now we must celebrate and rejoice, because your brother was dead and has come to life again; he was lost and has been found."

Luke 15:32

DISCUSS AS A FAMILY

• Talk about experiences of forgiving family members—and of being forgiven.

• Discuss any anxiety about talking to the priest when going to confession. Some nervousness is normal. It will go away quickly.

PRAY

Lord Jesus, have mercy on me, a sinner.

DO

Celebrate the Sacrament of Reconciliation as a family.

Visit **www.ChristOurLife.org/family** for more family resources.

God's Family Celebrates the Eucharist

CHAPTER 24

The Mass Is a Meal in Memory of Jesus

Families share meals together. God's family shares a special meal together. The eucharistic celebration, or Mass, is the special family meal of the Church. It is our best way to give praise and thanks to God. Catholics celebrate the Lord's Day by taking part in Mass on Sunday. They celebrate special occasions with the Eucharist.

When we celebrate the Mass, we remember that Jesus had a special meal with his friends before he died. At Jesus' Last Supper, he took bread and said:

> "Take this, all of you, and eat it: this is my body, which will be given up for you."
>
> from Eucharistic Prayer I

Then Jesus took the cup filled with wine. He thanked his Father, gave the apostles the cup, and said:

> "Take this, all of you, and drink from it: this is the cup of my blood. It will be shed for you and for all so that sins may be forgiven."
>
> from Eucharistic Prayer I

Jesus shared himself as food and drink with his apostles. He told them, "Do this in memory of me." From that time on, through his apostles and priests, Jesus has made himself present in the Eucharist. When Jesus becomes present in the bread and wine, we can share in his death and Resurrection.

165

The Mass Is a Sacrifice of Love

At every celebration of the Mass, Jesus shows his great love.

- He teaches us through the readings.
- He offers himself to God the Father for us.
- He makes us one with him and one with God's family in Holy Communion.
- He helps us become more like him so that we can bring his love into the world.
- He strengthens us to continue his work.

All over the world, Catholics celebrate the Eucharist. They remember Jesus and join in his sacrifice. They are united with him and with one another.

Jesus Remains with Us

Jesus is always with us. We can speak with him anytime that we wish. We can also visit him at church. He is in our churches in a special way, especially when we celebrate Mass.

Sometimes we hold a special prayer service to honor Jesus in the Eucharist. The priest gives us the **blessing** of Jesus with the sacred host. We call this blessing **benediction**. We bless ourselves by making the Sign of the Cross.

Some people cannot go to church because they are sick or dying. They can still receive Jesus in the Eucharist. People from the parish bring Holy Communion to them. The Eucharist strengthens them and reminds them that Jesus and the Church are with them.

A Moment with Jesus

Talk to Jesus in the quiet of your heart. Thank him for always being with you.

Jesus Teaches Us to Listen to Him

When Jesus lived on earth, he taught people the good news of salvation. One day Jesus went up a mountain and sat down to teach. The crowds listened to his words about his Father's love and how to live, but just hearing his words was not enough. Jesus wanted them to put his words into practice. So he ended with this story about two men who built houses.

"The first man built a house on rock. The rain fell, the floods came, and the winds blew hard against it. No harm was done to the house because it was built on rock. It was firm and strong. How wise the first man was to build his house on rock! The second man built a house on sand. The rain fell, the floods came, and the winds blew. His house fell and was completely ruined. How foolish the second man was to build his house on sand!"

Jesus explained the story:

"Everyone who listens to my words and acts on them will be like a wise man who built his house on rock. . . . And everyone who listens to these words of mine but does not act on them will be like a fool who built his house on sand."

adapted from Matthew 7:24–27

Jesus Speaks to Us at Mass

When God's family celebrates the Eucharist, Jesus is present. He is present in the priest, in his people, in his Word, and in the sacred bread and wine. He is present during the two main parts of the Mass: the **Liturgy of the Word** and the Liturgy of the Eucharist.

The Liturgy of the Word is the celebration of God's speaking to us. God himself teaches us through his words in the Bible.

A lector, or reader, does the first reading. It is from the Old Testament. We listen and say, "Thanks be to God." Then we pray a psalm. In Sunday Masses and on feast days, there is a second reading. Usually this reading is from one of the **epistles**, or letters, in the New Testament. All the readings for Mass are read from the **Lectionary**.

To welcome the Gospel, we stand and sing, "Alleluia." To show that Jesus speaks to us, we say, "Glory to you, Lord," as we make a cross on our foreheads, lips, and hearts.

We listen with our minds and hearts as the priest or deacon reads from the Gospel of Matthew, Mark, Luke, or John. Then we say, "Praise to you, Lord Jesus Christ."

A priest or deacon explains God's words in the **homily**. He tells us how to live them. When we keep God's words, we are like the wise man who built his house on rock.

Circle the five parts of the Liturgy of the Word that are God's Word to us.

Sharing Sunday

Marita is a busy mom. She works hard at her job and loves being with her family. She also helps out at church. Follow the directions to walk with Marita through her Sunday.

Marita Jones and her family go to church. Draw a path from their house to the church. Put a cross on the top of the church.

During Mass, they celebrate the Liturgy of the Word. Fill in the blanks:

- They pray _____ between the first and second readings.

- During the _____ , they listen to the priest explain God's word.

After Communion, the priest gives Marita a pyx to carry the consecrated host.

Marita brings Holy _____ to people who cannot get to Mass. Draw her path from the church to Mr. Malone's

apartment building and then to Mrs. Curson's house.

After visiting and praying with them, Marita stops at the park. Draw a path from Mrs. Curson's house to the park and draw some trees and flowers in the park.

Marita says a prayer of thanks to God. What things is she thankful for this morning?

Marita returns to the church and joins her family who are helping at the soup kitchen. Draw a path from the park to the church.

After church, the Jones family goes out together. Where do they go? Draw a path from the church to that place.

We Remember

Why did Jesus give us the Eucharist?
Jesus gave us the Eucharist so that we could join in his sacrifice to the Father and so that he could be with us as our spiritual food.

When do we hear the Word of God at Mass?
We hear the Word of God read and explained in the Scripture readings and in the homily during the Liturgy of the Word.

Words to Know
benediction	blessing
epistle	homily
Lectionary	Liturgy of the Word

We Respond

The promises of the Lord I will sing forever.

Psalm 89:2

Building Family Faith

CHAPTER SUMMARY The Mass is the great meal we share as God's family. We receive the risen Jesus' Body and Blood in the Eucharist, and hear his Word in the Scripture readings and the homily.

REFLECT
While they were eating, Jesus took bread, said the blessing, broke it, and giving it to his disciples said, "Take and eat; this is my body".
Matthew 26:26

DISCUSS AS A FAMILY
- The Mass is a meal. How is it like the meals we eat together as a family?
- Discuss those things for which we are grateful. What are we most grateful for today?
- How can we show our gratitude to Jesus for the Eucharist?

PRAY
Thank you, Lord Jesus, for giving us the gift of yourself in the Eucharist.

DO
Prepare for Sunday Mass by reading the Gospel together as a family.

Visit **www.ChristOurLife.org/family** for more family resources.

CHAPTER 25

The Eucharist Is a Gift

Gifts Show Love

Gifts speak. They say, "See, I love you!" The giver is loved more than the gift. Gifts help us celebrate our love for each other. Gifts help us be more aware of the love we have for each other.

God gives gifts to show us love. He has given us the beautiful world. We take his gifts of wheat and grapes and, through our work, change them into bread and wine. They are signs of ourselves. Then at Mass we bring them as gifts to God. God's family gives God what we are and what we make.

We Offer Our Gifts with Jesus

God also gives gifts to us at Mass. In the Liturgy of the Word, he gives us the gift of his words. God tells us how much he loves us and how to live as his loving children. In the Liturgy of the Eucharist, God gives us the gift of of his body and blood in Holy Communion.

Jesus gave himself as a perfect gift to his Father. He did everything to please God. He died on the cross to save us from sin. Jesus offers the gift of his sacrifice on the cross for all people at every Mass.

The **Liturgy of the Eucharist** is a special gift exchange. The priest takes our gifts of bread and wine and offers them to God. During the Mass, the bread and wine become the Body and Blood of Jesus Christ.

Then with Jesus, we offer ourselves to God the Father. We do this in the Eucharistic Prayer, especially when the priest says:

> "Through him, with him, in him,
> in the unity of the Holy Spirit,
> all glory and honor is yours,
> almighty Father, forever and ever."
>
> from Eucharistic Prayer I

We respond to this prayer by saying amen with great joy.

Then God gives us Jesus in Holy Communion as a gift of his love.

Gifts of Love

Print on each line the letter of the answer from the Word Bank. Answers can be used more than once.

WORD BANK

A. God the Father   D. ourselves
B. Jesus   E. love
C. his words

_____ 1. Why did God our Father give us the gift of his Son?

_____ 2. To whom do we offer gifts at Mass?

_____ 3. Who do our gifts of bread and wine become during Mass?

_____ 4. To whom did Jesus give the gift of himself when he died on the cross?

_____ 5. What gift does God give us in the Liturgy of the Word?

_____ 6. What gift do we receive in the Liturgy of the Eucharist?

_____ 7. At Mass what two gifts do we offer to God with Jesus?

At Mass we remember the dying and rising of Jesus. Jesus offers himself to the Father. We offer ourselves with him. We bring our prayers. We bring our joys and our sufferings. We bring all the good things we have done.

Jesus Makes Us One in Him

When Jesus gives himself to us as food and drink in the Holy Eucharist, we become one with him and his family, the Church. We are united with the Father and the Holy Spirit. We are united with Mary and all the angels and saints in heaven. We are united with everyone who shares the Eucharist on earth.

In a letter Saint Paul reminds us that Jesus makes us one in Holy Communion:

> Though we are many, we are one body because we all share in the one bread which is Jesus.

adapted from 1 Corinthians 10:17

In Holy Communion we come alive with the glorious life of Jesus. We become more like him. With his grace we can become better people. Then each time we take part in Mass, we can offer God a better gift.

> "Father, I pray that they may all be one as you and I are one."

adapted from John 17:20–21

Jesus Gives Us His Peace at Mass

During Mass God fills us with his life and love. God can use us then to bring his love and care to others. At the end of the Mass, the priest or deacon tells us, "Go in peace to love and serve the Lord."

We go out to share Christ's peace by loving others.

Liturgy of the Eucharist

Label the branches of the grape vine with the names of some of those who are united by the Holy Eucharist.

"I am the vine, you are the branches."

John 15:5

Peace Pledge

Find the missing words in the Dove of Peace. Write them on the lines.

joy

forgive

help

share

I will _____ food with those who are hungry.

I will _____ those who hurt me.

I will bring _____ to those who are sad.

I will _____ those in need.

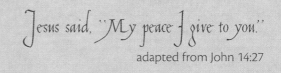

Jesus said, "My peace I give to you."

adapted from John 14:27

We Remember

What gifts do we offer God at the celebration of the Eucharist?

At the celebration of the Eucharist, with Jesus, we offer Jesus and ourselves to God.

Words to Know
Liturgy of the Eucharist

We Respond

May the Lord accept the sacrifice at your hands for the praise and glory of his name, for our good and the good of all his Church.

from the *Ordinary of the Mass*

Who Am I?

Write the letter of the answer next to each person's description of himself or herself.

A. Zacchaeus
B. Peter
C. the woman at Simon's house
D. Nicodemus
E. the rich young man

_____ 1. I washed Jesus' feet with my tears.

_____ 2. Jesus told me to sell all that I have and give the money to the poor.

_____ 3. I denied Jesus three times.

_____ 4. I climbed a tree to see Jesus.

_____ 5. Jesus told me "You must be born of water and Spirit to enter God's kingdom."

Reflecting the Light of God's Love

Write the Two Great Laws in the mirror:

Love _____

and Love _____

Help the Shepherd

Fill in the answers to the questions to help a shepherd find something he lost.

The sacrifice in which we remember
Jesus' death and Resurrection is called

__ __ __ ◯ .

The family of those who believe in
Jesus is called

__ ◯ __ __ __ __ .

The two main gifts we bring to
the altar are

__ __ ◯ __ __

and __ __ __ ◯ .

The gift that Jesus gives us when
he forgives us is

◯ __ __ __ __ .

**Now place the circled letters in order
in the spaces below.**

__ __ __ __ __

A House Built on Rock

Find and circle the following words:

Liturgy of the Eucharist	First reading	Psalm	Body	Baptism
Holy Communion	Benediction	Gospel	Penance	
Homily	Second Reading	Blood	Bread	
Liturgy of the Word	Reconciliation	Wine	Peace	

```
S R G Y L M L Q U B A P T I S M A S R O I
M D O M G A I K U S V H S D W L C E E X G
G J S F C Z T G P S A L M H H O F C C S P
R H P C R L U Z X N Z K P Y O L P O O Y V
I G E M H W R P E N A N C E L J O N N I R
T K L S F V G H P Q I U F B Y H K D C F Q
L I T U R G Y O F T H E E U C H A R I S T
H X H F D F O H S Y T V M T O O Z E L F G
D B O D Y G F E P E A C E K M M X A I Y P
W L B N G W T V A J S L V W M I K D A W V
U O Q N J X H B O Z U S B X U L H I T I H
P O K B E N E D I C T I O N N Y P N I N T
R D Z P S O W Z J L X E L O I P G G O E U
S S Y H B X O U H B W S G Q O H P O N B K
S F I R S T R E A D I N G P N L B R E A D
L D N D O H D X N H L A Q Z E F Y I G F Q
```

Celebrating Our Life with Jesus

Song

First Reading

Reader: A reading from the First Letter to the Corinthians

The cup of blessing that we bless, is it not a participation in the blood of Christ? The bread that we break, is it not a participation in the body of Christ? Because the loaf of bread is one, we, though many, are one body, for we all partake of the one loaf.

1 Corinthians 10:16–17

The Word of the Lord.

Response: Thanks be to God.

Psalm

Response: You are my God. I call on your name.

Side 1: O God, you are my God—I long for you! My body yearns for you; my soul is thirsty for you, like land that is dry, lifeless, and without water.

Side 2: So I look to you in the sanctuary to see your power and glory.

For your love is better than life itself; my lips shall give you praise!

Side 1: I will bless you as long as I live; I will lift up my hands, calling on your name.

Side 2: My soul shall savor the rich feast of praise, with joyous lips my mouth shall honor you!

Side 1: When I think of you as I go to my bed, through the night watches I will recall

That you indeed are my help, and in the shadow of your wings I shout for joy.

Side 2: My soul holds fast to you; your right hand carries me.

adapted from Psalm 63:2–9

Gospel

Reader: A reading from the Gospel according to John

So Jesus said to them, "I am the living bread that came down from heaven; whoever eats this bread will live forever; and the bread that I will give is my flesh for the life of the world.

"Whoever eats my flesh and drinks my blood has eternal life, and I will raise him on the last day.

"Just as the living Father sent me and I have life because of the Father, so also the one who feeds on me will have life because of me.

"This is the bread that came down from heaven. Unlike your ancestors who ate and still died, whoever eats this bread will live forever."

adapted from John 6:51–58

The Gospel of the Lord.

Response: Praise to you, Lord Jesus.

Reflection

Intercessions

Response: O Lord, hear our prayer.

Song

Family Feature

Seeing the Sacred in the Ordinary

As Catholics, we treasure the crucifixes, statues, medals, pictures, and other sacred objects in our churches and homes because they help us get in touch with God. But commonplace things and ordinary actions can be sacred too. Nothing is too small or too humble to reflect the love of God. Learning to see the sacred in the everyday objects and actions of our lives is one of the most important parts of religious education—for you and for your child.

To see the sacred in the ordinary, we need to see the world with sacramental eyes—the eyes of faith. In the sacraments, God comes to us in ordinary things—the water of Baptism, the bread and wine of the Eucharist, the oil of Confirmation. In this Family Feature you will find some ideas to help your family recognize the sacred in your daily lives.

"Blessed are the eyes that see what you see."

Luke 10:23

Water of Baptism

Oil of Confirmation ❯

❮ The Sacrament of Matrimony

Bread and wine of the Eucharist

180a

Family Feature

Name some sacred objects.

Ask family members to think about the objects in your home that hold a special meaning for them. Ask each person to tell about one of the objects and why it helps him or her feel connected to God. Don't limit your selections to holy items like crucifixes or religious artwork on the walls, but instead open your eyes to the spiritual meaning of ordinary things. Your sacred object may be the dining room table, where the family shares meals and stories of the day. Another family member may choose the family photos on the mantle or the flowers in the garden. The grill where Dad cooked hot dogs for your child's birthday party might also be a sacred object.

Visit **www.ChristOurLife.org/family** for more family resources.

Create sacred places.

Create a quiet place in your home free of television, computers, and other distractions—a place where people read, pray, relax, and talk quietly. Single out a bench on your deck or a chair in a quiet corner of your house as a special place where people can go to connect with God. You could also make the door of your refrigerator a holy place adorned with family photos, inspiring text, photos and mementos from the charities your family supports.

Be alert to sacred time.

The time that we have is a gift from God. Be mindful that God is always present in it; he abides in every second. The activities of daily life can seem to be a never-ending succession of tasks and errands, but they are also invitations to connect with a God who loves us. All you need to do is pull your mind away from thoughts about what you need to do tomorrow or what went wrong last week, and focus on the present moment. God is in it.

Help your child do this by paying attention to the time the family has together.

For example, here's a way to increase your mindfulness and make your mealtimes special. Before everyone digs into the food, stop for a moment and say a prayer of gratitude for all the people who made the meal possible: the farmers, the food workers, the transporters, the people who work at the grocery, the family members who shopped for the food and earned the money to pay for it. After thinking of all those people, you can hold hands and say your normal grace before meals together.

Family Feature

Finding God in All Things

Look at this picture of a family room. It is filled with many objects that might be sacred to the family who lives there. Try to see each object with sacramental eyes and think of ways it can reflect the love of God.

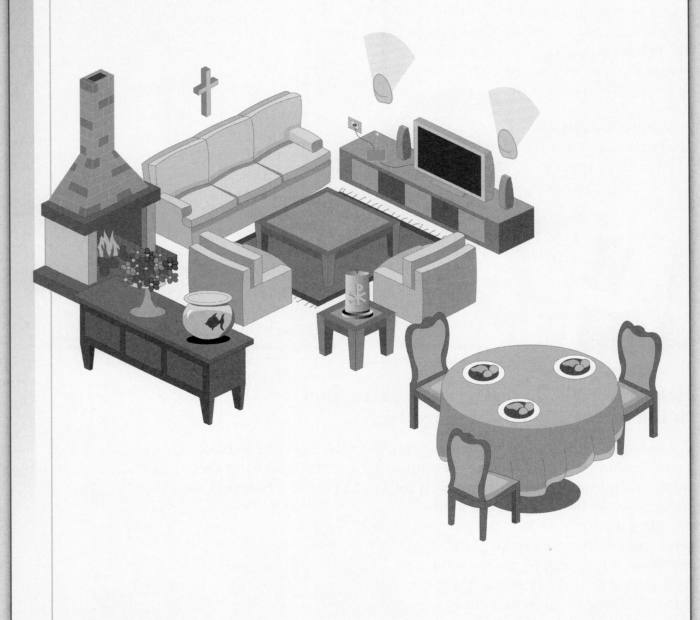

Special Seasons and Lessons

The Year in Our Church

Advent · Christmas · Ordinary Time · Lent · Holy Week · Easter

Epiphany

Ash Wednesday

Christmas

Easter Sunday

First Sunday of Advent

Feast of All Saints

Winter · Spring · Fall · Summer

Pentacost

Ordinary Time

Liturgical Calendar

The liturgical calendar highlights the feast days and seasons of the Church year. Various colors symbolize the different seasons.

1|All Saints and All Souls

We Are United in the Communion of Saints

In the Communion of Saints, we are united with all people who belong to Christ, including those who have died. In November, we celebrate two days that help us to remember and strengthen this bond of love.

Honoring the Saints

On November 1, All Saints Day, we honor all of the saints. The saints are the members of our family of faith who are living now with God in heaven. We remember those people that the Church has officially named as saints. We also remember the many unknown people who loved God and lived holy lives. They too are saints.

My Favorite Saints

Write the names of your favorite saints.

_____

_____

_____

What do you most admire about these saints?

_____

_____

_____

How will you follow their example of holiness in your own life?

_____

_____

_____

_____

❮ Saint Francis of Assisi and Mary

183

We Pray for All Souls

On November 2, All Souls Day, we pray for those who have died who are on their way to heaven. We say that these souls are in purgatory. In purgatory, those people who died in God's love are cleansed of all remaining sin so that they can live forever with God in heaven. We pray for them to help speed their journey to God.

This is a prayer we can say for those who have died:

> Eternal rest grant to them, O Lord, and let perpetual light shine upon them. May they rest in peace. Amen.
>
> Roman Breviary

We Honor Those Who Have Died

There are many different ways that people honor those who have died. In many Latin American countries and in the Philippines, All Souls Day, or the Day of the Dead, is a feast day and a public holiday.

In Mexico, people light candles and kneel at the graves of their departed family members. The graves are decorated with flowers, and the family brings food to eat a meal in the presence of their loved ones again.

In the Philippines, candles are burned at graves for nine days in preparation for the feast. Graves are trimmed and weeded, and the tombstones cleaned and painted. On the evening of All Souls, young people go from door to door impersonating the holy souls freed from purgatory and on their way to heaven. They ask for gifts of candy, cookies, and other pastries.

How Do We Honor Them?

What are some other ways that people honor family members who have died?

_____

_____

_____

_____

_____

_____

The Saints and Holy Souls Help Us

The saints in heaven pray for us, and the example of their lives helps us to follow Christ more faithfully. We pray for the souls in purgatory, helping them on their journey to God. The souls in purgatory also pray for us. We look forward to the day when we will all celebrate God's love together in heaven.

3 | Christmas

Act One

(Two shepherd children enter, one holding a lamb. Sarah, a little girl carrying a puppy, comes to meet them.)

Shepherd 1: Where have you been, Sarah?

Sarah: My friend Rachel just gave me this beautiful puppy. I have always wanted my very own pet!

Shepherd 2: *(Sadly)* Too bad you missed it all.

Sarah: *(Excitedly)* What? What are you two talking about?

Shepherd 1: The baby with the beautiful lady and the kind man!

Shepherd 2: And the music! You should have heard that wonderful music!

Sarah: Music? Out here? Where did it come from?

Shepherd 1: From angels.

Shepherd 2: Angels from heaven!

Sarah: Angels from heaven? Tell me what happened!

Act Two

(The two shepherds and Sarah sit down on the floor to watch as the readers and characters report on what happened. Choir sings "O Little Town of Bethlehem.")

Reader 1: Now it came to pass that Caesar Augustus sent forth an order to all people in the land.

Messenger: *(Gruffly)* Every man must go register in the town in which he was born.

Reader 2: So Joseph and Mary set out from Nazareth to go to the town of David, called Bethlehem. When they arrived, they immediately tried to find shelter, for it was almost time for Jesus to be born.

Innkeeper 1: No room!

Innkeeper 2: Sorry, no room.

Innkeeper 3: We're filled. No room!

Innkeeper 4: There's a stable over there if you want to use it.

(Mary and Joseph walk toward the stable and kneel beside the manger. Choir sings "Away in a Manger.")

Reader 1: There were shepherds on the hillside tending their sheep. Suddenly an angel of the Lord stood by them.

(Angel appears with arms extended.)

Angel: Behold, I bring you good news of great joy! Today in the town of Bethlehem a Savior has been born. He is Christ the Lord. And here is a sign for you: you will find the baby wrapped in swaddling clothes and lying in a manger. *(Angel stands behind the manger.)*

Readers 1 and 2: *(Loudly)* And suddenly there was with the angel a host of angels praising God and singing.

(Choir sings "Angels We Have Heard on High," beginning with chorus.)

Act Three

Shepherds: Let's go and see this wonderful sight again! *(They walk slowly to the manger. One child sings first verse of "Silent Night" as class hums. Everyone sings other verses.)*

Sarah: *(Standing facing the others)* Oh! What shall I give him? *(She joyfully walks over and gives her puppy to Joseph.)*

Reader 1: What will you give him?

Reader 2: What will you give him?

Mary: *(Standing and holding up Jesus)* Give him your heart.

(All sing "O Come, All Ye Faithful.")

4 | Lent

Spring is a time of new life. During spring, the Church prepares to celebrate the new life Jesus gives to us. This season of preparation is called Lent. The word *Lent* means "springtime."

During Lent, we remember our Baptism and renew our commitment to live the new life Jesus gave to us. We celebrate the Sacrament of Penance and Reconciliation. We prepare to celebrate the Paschal Mystery—Jesus' suffering, death, Resurrection, and Ascension.

During Lent, adults and children prepare to be baptized at Easter. Those preparing for Baptism are called *catechumens*.

The season of Lent begins on Ash Wednesday. The priest blesses ashes and traces the Sign of the Cross on our foreheads. We promise to turn away from sin and remain faithful to the Gospel.

> Come back to me with all your hearts.
> Turn to the Lord your God.
>
> (adapted from Joel 2:12–13)

During Lent, we pray, we fast, and we give alms. We change our hearts to become better Christians. In each section below, write what you will do during Lent to change your heart and turn to the Lord.

Prayer

We pray daily. We read the Bible. We ask God to forgive us our sins.

During Lent, I will *pray every night* .

Fasting

We choose not to eat certain foods, especially treats, and not to take part in certain activities that we otherwise enjoy. We do not eat meat on Ash Wednesday or on Fridays during Lent. We make these sacrifices to show love for God and others.

During Lent, I will *give up ice cream* .

Almsgiving

We share what we have with people in need. We do good deeds for others.

During Lent, I will *make sweters* .

5 | Holy Week

Throughout Lent, we prepare for Easter. We remember the great love Jesus showed for us when he accepted death on the cross.

During the last week of Lent, called Holy Week, we make our final preparations. We gather at church to pray. We follow Jesus on his way of the cross. We remember Jesus' passion and death. We wait in hope for Easter, the celebration of Jesus' Resurrection. In all these ways, we celebrate the Paschal Mystery.

Following Jesus During Holy Week

There are many ways that we can follow Jesus more closely during Holy Week. We can pray the Stations of the Cross. We can pray the Sorrowful Mysteries of the Rosary. We can celebrate the liturgies of Holy Week.

Palm (Passion) Sunday

On Palm (Passion) Sunday, we remember how a great crowd of people hailed Jesus as their king when he rode into Jerusalem. They waved palm branches and shouted "Hosanna to the Son of David." (Matthew 21:9) At church, we receive blessed palms and walk in procession as a sign that we want Jesus to be our king. We hear the Gospel about Jesus' death on the cross. After Mass, we take the palms home. We can display them near a cross or crucifix. Each time we look at the palm, we can pray "Praise and honor to you, Lord Jesus Christ, King of endless glory."

The Liturgies of the Easter Triduum

Holy Thursday

At the Last Supper, Jesus gave us the gift of himself in the Holy Eucharist. Jesus also washed his disciples' feet. Every year on Holy Thursday, there is a special Mass of the Lord's Supper. We remember Jesus' great love and thank him for giving us himself in the Eucharist. After this Mass, the priest carries the Blessed Sacrament in procession to a special place decorated with flowers and candles. Until midnight, people continue to adore the Blessed Sacrament and thank Jesus for the gift of the Eucharist.

Good Friday

On Good Friday, the Church remembers the day Jesus died to take away our sins. We listen to the reading from the Gospel of John about Jesus' sufferings and death.

We offer special prayers for the Church and for people everywhere. During the service, a cross is carried in procession and is honored. We may kiss the cross to show our love for Jesus. Good Friday is the only day of the year on which Mass is not celebrated, but there is a communion service in which we may receive Jesus in Holy Communion and thank him for his great love in suffering for us.

Easter Vigil and Easter

Easter is not simply one feast among many. It is *the* feast of the year because it is when we joyously celebrate the Resurrection of our Lord. We can truly celebrate Easter once we have prepared our hearts during Lent and Holy Week.

The Sorrowful Mysteries of the Rosary

The Sorrowful Mysteries of the Rosary tell the story of Jesus' suffering and death for our salvation. When we pray the Rosary, we thank Jesus for his great gift of love.

Choose one of the Sorrowful Mysteries of the Rosary. Read the Scripture passage that tells the story of that mystery. Draw a picture of the mystery. Remember Jesus' great love for you.

The Agony in the Garden
Matthew 26:36–46

The Crowning with Thorns
Mark 15:16–20

The Death of Our Lord
(The Crucifixion)
Mark 15:33–39

The Scourging
Matthew 27:15–26

The Carrying of the Cross
Mark 15:21–25

6 | Easter

Easter is the most important day of the Church year. It is the day we celebrate Jesus' Resurrection. It begins the 50-day season of Easter in which we celebrate the Ascension of our Lord and Pentecost. The Easter season is a wonderful time to pray the Glorious Mysteries of the Rosary.

The Story of Jesus' Resurrection

On the morning of the first day of the week, the women went to Jesus' tomb to anoint his body. They found Jesus' tomb empty. The angels at the tomb told them that Jesus had been raised from the dead. They were amazed at what they saw and heard. They did not yet understand what it all meant.

Then Jesus himself appeared to his disciples and helped them to understand. At first, the disciples did not recognize Jesus. As Jesus appeared to them, they came to recognize him and to believe that Jesus is Lord.

After 40 days, Jesus was taken up to heaven. We call this the Ascension of the Lord. Jesus told his disciples to wait in Jerusalem. He was going to send them the Holy Spirit, just as he had promised.

adapted from Luke 24

We Celebrate Easter

At Easter, we are happy because Jesus promised to be with us always.

We sing and pray,

"Alleluia! Jesus is risen."

An Easter Prayer

Procession

Prayer

Catechist: God our Father, as we think about the risen Jesus in this celebration, help us realize that he lives with us and in us and that he gives us his peace and joy. We ask this through Christ our Lord.

All: Amen

Reading *(adapted from Luke 24:1–12)*

Reader: Early Sunday morning Mary of Magdala and some other holy women went to the tomb to anoint the body of Jesus. *(Women walk toward tomb.)* When they arrived, they found the stone rolled back.

Mary: Look! The tomb is open. I wonder who rolled the heavy stone away. *(Women go inside.)*

Reader: The women went inside but did not find Jesus' body anywhere in the tomb. The women were puzzled. Then they saw two angels dressed in brilliant clothes.

Angel: Why do you look among the dead for someone alive? Jesus is not here. He has been raised. Remember that he told you he would be crucified but would rise again on the third day.

Reader: Then the women ran back to tell the other disciples. Peter ran to the tomb to see for himself. He was amazed by what had happened.

The Gospel of the Lord.

All: Praise to you, Lord Jesus Christ.

Song

Prayers *(All sing "Alleluia" after each prayer.)*

Leader 1: Jesus is risen! He shares his life with us.

Leader 2: God, who raised Jesus from the dead, will raise us too.

Leader 3: Christ has freed us from the power of sin and death.

Leader 4: Now we can walk in the light of the Lord.

Petitions

All: Lord, hear our prayer.

Song

7 | Pentecost

Fifty days after Easter, we celebrate Pentecost Sunday. On Pentecost, we celebrate Jesus' gift of the Holy Spirit. We also recall how the Holy Spirit was given to Jesus' disciples.

After they received the gift of the Holy Spirit, Jesus' disciples continued the work that Jesus had begun. They taught others about Jesus and about the Kingdom of God that Jesus had announced. Through the gift of the Holy Spirit, the disciples gave witness to Jesus in their words and in their actions.

Peter's Marvelous Deed

One day, when Peter and John were going to the Temple in Jerusalem to pray, they saw a man at the gate who had been unable to walk from birth. This man called out to them, begging for money.

Peter looked at the man and said, "I have neither silver nor gold, but what I do have I give you: in the name of Jesus Christ the Nazorean, walk." Peter then took the man's hand and helped him stand up.

The man leapt up. He walked and jumped and praised God. The people in the Temple recognized the man as the one who often begged at the entrance gate. They were amazed and astonished that this man had been healed.

adapted from Acts of the Apostles 3:1–10

The Holy Spirit at Work Today

The gift of the Holy Spirit helps the Church to continue the work of Jesus today. This is the mission of the Church: to tell people about salvation through Jesus' life, death, and Resurrection. The Church gives witness to Jesus. The Church passes on to others, by words and actions, the faith that we have received from the apostles. The Holy Spirit guides the Church to proclaim the Kingdom of God.

We received the gift of the Holy Spirit at our Baptism. Through the gift of the Holy Spirit, we share in the mission of the Church. The Holy Spirit helps us to proclaim the good news of salvation. The Holy Spirit helps us to continue the work of Jesus. We give witness to our faith in Jesus through our words and our actions.

Come, Holy Spirit,

Fill the hearts of your faithful,

And kindle in them

The fire of your love.

What Catholics Should Know

(continued next page)

(continued from previous page)

Prayer and How We Pray

God is always with us. He wants us to talk to him and listen to him. In prayer we raise our hearts and minds to God. We are able to speak to and listen to God because through the Holy Spirit, God teaches us how to pray.

We Pray in Many Ways

Since prayer is so important, the Church teaches us to pray often and in many different ways. Sometimes we bless or adore God (prayer of blessing and adoration). Other times we ask God for something for ourselves (prayer of petition). Sometimes we pray for others (prayer of intercession). We also thank God in prayer (prayer of thanksgiving). Finally, we can also praise God (prayer of praise). We can pray alone or with others. We can pray silently or out loud.

We Meditate and Contemplate

One way to pray is to meditate. To meditate is to think about God. We try to keep our attention and focus on God. In meditation we may use Scripture, prayer books, or icons, which are religious images, to help us concentrate and spark our imagination.

Another way to pray is to contemplate. This means that we rest quietly in God's presence.

We Get Ready to Pray

We live in a busy, noisy, and fast-paced world. Because of this, we can have difficulty concentrating. In order to meditate or reflect, we need to prepare ourselves. We can get ready for meditation by moving our bodies into a comfortable position, sitting with our backs straight and both feet on the floor. We can close our eyes, fold our hands in front of us, take a deep breath, and then slowly let it out. We can establish a rhythm by slowly counting to three while breathing in and slowly counting to three while breathing out. Concentrating on our breathing helps us quiet our thoughts.

We Avoid Distractions

If we become distracted by thinking about something such as the day at school or a sporting event, we can just go back to thinking about our breathing. After a little practice, we will be able to avoid distractions, pray with our imagination, and spend time with God or Jesus in our hearts.

Prayers We Pray as Catholics

We can pray with any words that come to mind. Sometimes when we find that choosing our own words is difficult, we can use traditional prayers. Memorizing traditional prayers such as the following can be very helpful. When we memorize prayers, we take them to heart, meaning that we not only learn the words, but also try to understand and live them. See the inside front and back covers of your books for the most frequently used prayers.

Hail, Holy Queen

Hail, holy Queen, Mother of mercy,
hail, our life, our sweetness, and our hope.
To you we cry, the children of Eve;
to you we send up our sighs,
mourning and weeping in this land
    of exile.
Turn, then, most gracious advocate,
your eyes of mercy toward us;
lead us home at last
and show us the blessed fruit of
    your womb, Jesus:
O clement, O loving, O sweet
    Virgin Mary.

The Angelus

Verse. The angel of the Lord declared unto Mary.

Response. And she conceived of the Holy Spirit.
Hail Mary . . .

Verse. Behold the handmaid of the Lord.

Response. May it be done unto me according to your word.
Hail Mary . . .

Verse. And the Word was made flesh.

Response. And dwelt among us.
Hail Mary . . .

Verse. Pray for us, O holy Mother of God.

Response. That we may be made worthy of the promises of Christ.

Let us pray.
Lord,
fill our hearts with your grace:
once, through the message of an angel
you revealed to us the incarnation of
    your Son;
now, through his suffering and death
lead us to the glory of his resurrection.
We ask this through Christ our Lord.

Amen.

Nicene Creed

We believe in one God,
    the Father, the Almighty,
    maker of heaven and earth,
    of all that is seen and unseen.
We believe in one Lord, Jesus Christ,
    the only Son of God,
    eternally begotten of the Father,
    God from God, Light from Light,
    true God from true God,
    begotten, not made, one in Being
        with the Father.
    Through him all things were made.
    For us men and for our salvation
        he came down from heaven:
by the power of the Holy Spirit
    he was born of the Virgin Mary,
        and became man.
For our sake he was crucified under
        Pontius Pilate;
    he suffered, died, and was buried.
    On the third day he rose again

in fulfillment of the Scriptures;
    he ascended into heaven
        and is seated at the right hand of
            the Father.
He will come again in glory to judge
        the living and the dead,
    and his kingdom will have no end.
We believe in the Holy Spirit, the Lord,
    the giver of life,
    who proceeds from the Father
        and the Son.
    With the Father and the Son he is
        worshiped and glorified.
    He has spoken through the Prophets.
    We believe in one holy catholic and
        apostolic Church.
    We acknowledge one baptism for the
        forgiveness of sins.
    We look for the resurrection of the dead,
        and the life of the world to come.
            Amen.

Pope Benedict XVI has suggested that certain prayers that are shared by the universal Church could be learned in Latin and prayed as a sign of the universal nature of the Church. English versions of the prayers below appear on the inside front cover of this book.

Pope Benedict XVI.

Signum Crucis (Sign of the Cross)

In nomine Patris,
et Filii,
et Spiritus Sancti.
Amen.

Gloria Patri (Glory Be to the Father)

Gloria Patri,
et Filio,
et Spiritui Sancto.
Sicut erat in principio,
et nunc, et semper,
Et in saecula saeculorum.
Amen.

Pater Noster (Our Father)

Pater noster, qui es in caelis,
sanctificetur nomen tuum.
Adveniat regnum tuum.
Fiat voluntas tua,
sicut in caelo et in terra.
Panem nostrum quotidianum da nobis hodie,
et dimitte nobis debita nostra
sicut et nos dimittimus debitoribus nostris.
Et ne nos inducas in tentationem,
sed libera nos a malo.
Amen.

Ave Maria (Hail Mary)

Ave Maria, gratia plena,
Dominus tecum.
Benedicta tu in mulieribus,
et benedictus fructus ventris tui, Iesus.
Sancta Maria, Mater Dei, ora pro nobis peccatoribus,
nunc, et in hora mortis nostrae.
Amen.

Upon entering a church, a boy makes the Sign of the Cross after dipping his fingers in holy water. Catholics make the Sign of the Cross during Mass and at other times as well.

The Rosary

The Rosary helps us pray to Jesus through Mary. When we pray the Rosary, we think about the special events, or mysteries, in the lives of Jesus and Mary.

The Rosary is made up of a string of beads and a crucifix. We hold the crucifix in our hands as we pray the Sign of the Cross. Then we pray the Apostles' Creed. Next to the crucifix, there is a single bead, followed by a set of three beads and another single bead. We pray the Lord's Prayer as we hold the first single bead and a Hail Mary at each bead in the set of three that follows. Then we pray the Glory Be to the Father. On the next single bead we think about the first mystery and pray the Lord's Prayer.

There are five sets of 10 beads; each set is called a decade. We pray a Hail Mary on each bead of a decade as we reflect on a particular mystery in the lives of Jesus and Mary. The Glory Be to the Father is prayed at the end of each set. Between sets is a single bead on which we think about one of the mysteries and pray the Lord's Prayer.

Our Lady of the Rosary, stained glass, Correze, France.

We end by holding the crucifix in our hands as we pray the Sign of the Cross.

PRAYING THE ROSARY

10. Think about the fourth mystery. Pray the Lord's Prayer.

9. Pray 10 Hail Marys and one Glory Be to the Father.

11. Pray 10 Hail Marys and one Glory Be to the Father.

8. Think about the third mystery. Pray the Lord's Prayer.

12. Think about the fifth mystery. Pray the Lord's Prayer.

7. Pray 10 Hail Marys and one Glory Be to the Father.

6. Think about the second mystery. Pray the Lord's Prayer.

5. Pray 10 Hail Marys and one Glory Be to the Father.

4. Think about the first mystery. Pray the Lord's Prayer.

13. Pray 10 Hail Marys and one Glory Be to the Father.

14. Pray the Hail, Holy Queen.

3. Pray three Hail Marys and one Glory Be to the Father.

2. Pray the Lord's Prayer.

15. Pray the Sign of the Cross.

1. Pray the Sign of the Cross and the Apostles' Creed.

Mysteries of the Rosary

The Church had three sets of mysteries for many centuries. In 2002 Pope John Paul II proposed a fourth set of mysteries—the Mysteries of Light, or the Luminous Mysteries. According to his suggestion, the four sets of mysteries might be prayed on the following days: the Joyful Mysteries on Monday and Saturday, the Sorrowful Mysteries on Tuesday and Friday, the Glorious Mysteries on Wednesday and Sunday, and the Luminous Mysteries on Thursday.

Pope John Paul II.

The Joyful Mysteries

1. *The Annunciation.* Mary learns she has been chosen to be the mother of Jesus.

2. *The Visitation.* Mary visits Elizabeth, who tells her that she is blessed among women.

3. *The Nativity.* Jesus is born in a stable in Bethlehem.

4. *The Presentation.* Mary and Joseph take the infant Jesus to the Temple to present him to God.

5. *The Finding of Jesus in the Temple.* Jesus is found in the Temple, discussing his faith with the teachers.

The Luminous Mysteries

1. *The Baptism of Jesus in the River Jordan.* God proclaims that Jesus is his beloved Son.

2. *The Wedding Feast at Cana.* At Mary's request, Jesus performs his first miracle.

3. *The Proclamation of the Kingdom of God.* Jesus calls all to conversion and service to the kingdom.

4. *The Transfiguration of Jesus.* Jesus is revealed in glory to Peter, James, and John.

5. *The Institution of the Eucharist.* Jesus gives us his Body and Blood at the Last Supper.

The Sorrowful Mysteries

1. *The Agony in the Garden.* Jesus prays in the garden of Gethsemane on the night before he dies.

2. *The Scourging at the Pillar.* Jesus is beaten with whips.

3. *The Crowning with Thorns.* Jesus is mocked and crowned with thorns.

4. *The Carrying of the Cross.* Jesus carries the cross on which he will be crucified.

5. *The Crucifixion.* Jesus is nailed to the cross and dies.

The Glorious Mysteries

1. *The Resurrection.* God the Father raises Jesus from the dead.

2. *The Ascension.* Jesus returns to his Father in heaven.

3. *The Coming of the Holy Spirit.* The Holy Spirit comes to bring new life to the disciples.

4. *The Assumption of Mary.* At the end of her life on earth, Mary is taken body and soul into heaven.

5. *The Coronation of Mary.* Mary is crowned as queen of heaven and earth.

Stations of the Cross

The 14 Stations of the Cross represent events from Jesus' passion and death. At each station, we use our senses and our imagination to reflect prayerfully on Jesus' suffering, death, and Resurrection.

1. Jesus Is Condemned to Death.
Pontius Pilate condemns Jesus to death.

2. Jesus Takes Up His Cross.
Jesus willingly accepts and patiently bears his cross.

3. Jesus Falls the First Time.
Weakened by torments and loss of blood, Jesus falls beneath his cross.

4. Jesus Meets His Sorrowful Mother.
Jesus meets his mother, Mary, who is filled with grief.

5. Simon of Cyrene Helps Jesus Carry the Cross.
Soldiers force Simon of Cyrene to carry the cross.

6. Veronica Wipes the Face of Jesus.
Veronica steps through the crowd to wipe the face of Jesus.

7. Jesus Falls a Second Time.
Jesus falls beneath the weight of the cross a second time.

8. Jesus Meets the Women of Jerusalem.
Jesus tells the women to weep not for him, but for themselves and for their children.

9. Jesus Falls the Third Time.
Weakened almost to the point of death, Jesus falls a third time.

10. Jesus Is Stripped of His Garments.
The soldiers strip Jesus of his garments, treating him as a common criminal.

11. Jesus Is Nailed to the Cross.
Jesus' hands and feet are nailed to the cross.

12. Jesus Dies on the Cross.
After suffering greatly on the cross, Jesus bows his head and dies.

13. Jesus Is Taken Down from the Cross.
The lifeless body of Jesus is tenderly placed in the arms of Mary, his mother.

14. Jesus Is Laid in the Tomb.
Jesus' disciples place his body in the tomb.

The closing prayer—sometimes included as a 15th station—reflects on the Resurrection of Jesus.

Celebrating and Living Our Catholic Faith

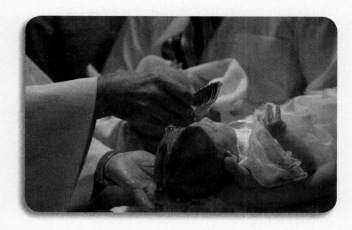

The Seven Sacraments

Jesus touches our lives through the sacraments. Our celebrations of the sacraments are signs of Jesus' presence in our lives and a means for receiving his grace. The Church celebrates seven sacraments, which are divided into three categories.

Sacraments of Initiation

These sacraments lay the foundation of every Christian life.

Baptism
In Baptism we receive new life in Christ. Baptism takes away original sin and gives us new birth in the Holy Spirit. Its signs are the pouring of water and calling on the Trinity.

Confirmation
Confirmation seals our life of faith in Jesus. Its signs are the laying of hands on a person's head, most often by a bishop, and the anointing with oil. Like Baptism, Confirmation is received only once.

Eucharist
The Eucharist nourishes our life of faith. Its signs are the bread and wine we receive—the Body and Blood of Christ.

Sacraments of Healing

These sacraments celebrate the healing power of Jesus.

Penance and Reconciliation
Through this sacrament we receive God's forgiveness. Forgiveness requires being sorry for our sins. In Reconciliation we receive Jesus' healing grace through absolution by the priest. The signs of this sacrament are the confession of sins and the words of absolution.

Anointing of the Sick
This sacrament unites a sick person's suffering with that of Jesus and brings forgiveness of sins. Oil, a symbol of strength, is the sign of this sacrament. A person is anointed with oil and receives the laying on of hands from a priest.

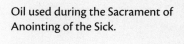

Oil used during the Sacrament of Anointing of the Sick.

Sacraments at the Service of Communion

These sacraments help members serve the community.

Holy Orders

In Holy Orders men are ordained as priests, deacons, or bishops. Priests serve as leaders of their communities, and deacons serve to remind us of our baptismal call to help others. Bishops carry on the teachings of the apostles. The signs of this sacrament are the laying on of hands and anointing with chrism by a bishop.

Matrimony

In Matrimony a man and woman are united with each other as a sign of the unity between Jesus and his Church. Matrimony requires the consent of the couple as expressed in the marriage promises. The couple and their wedding rings are the signs of this sacrament.

Order of the Mass

Sunday is the day on which we celebrate the Resurrection of Jesus. Sunday is the Lord's Day. We gather for Mass, rest from work, and perform works of mercy.

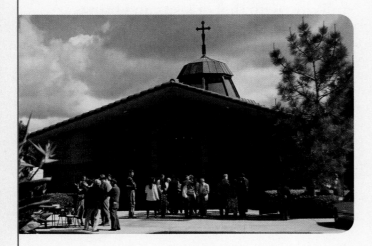

People all over the world gather at God's eucharistic table as brothers and sisters.

The Mass is the high point of the Christian life, and it follows a set order.

Introductory Rite—preparing to celebrate the Eucharist

- *Entrance Procession*—We gather as a community and praise God in song.

- *Sign of the Cross and Greeting*—We pray the Sign of the Cross. The priest welcomes us.

- *Penitential Rite*—We remember our sins and ask God for mercy.

- *Gloria*—We praise God in song.

- *Opening Prayer*—We ask God to hear our prayers.

Liturgy of the Word—hearing God's plan of salvation

- *First Reading*—We listen to God's Word, usually from the Old Testament.

- *Responsorial Psalm*—We respond to God's Word in song.

- *Second Reading*—We listen to God's Word from the New Testament.

- *Alleluia or Gospel Acclamation*—We sing "Alleluia!" (except during Lent) to praise God for the Good News.

- *Gospel*—We stand and listen to the Gospel of the Lord.

- *Homily*—The priest or the deacon explains God's Word.

- *Profession of Faith*—We proclaim our faith through the Nicene Creed.

- *General Intercessions*—We pray for our needs and the needs of others.

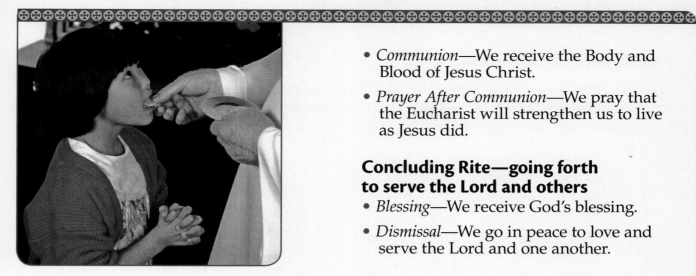

Liturgy of the Eucharist—celebrating Jesus' presence in the Eucharist

- *Preparation of the Altar and the Gifts*—We bring gifts of bread and wine to the altar.

- *Prayer over the Gifts*—The priest prays that God will accept our sacrifice.

- *Eucharistic Prayer*—This prayer of thanksgiving is the center and high point of the entire celebration.

- *Preface*—We give thanks and praise to God.

- *Holy, Holy*—We sing an acclamation of praise.

- *Consecration*—The bread and wine become the Body and Blood of Jesus Christ.

- *Memorial Acclamation*—We proclaim the mystery of our faith.

- *Great Amen*—We affirm the words and actions of the eucharistic prayer.

- *Communion Rite*—We prepare to receive the Body and Blood of Jesus Christ.

- *Lord's Prayer*—We pray the Our Father, or the Lord's Prayer.

- *Sign of Peace*—We offer one another Christ's peace.

- *Breaking of the Bread and the Lamb of God*—We pray for forgiveness, mercy, and peace.

- *Communion*—We receive the Body and Blood of Jesus Christ.

- *Prayer After Communion*—We pray that the Eucharist will strengthen us to live as Jesus did.

Concluding Rite—going forth to serve the Lord and others

- *Blessing*—We receive God's blessing.

- *Dismissal*—We go in peace to love and serve the Lord and one another.

Holy Days of Obligation

Holy Days of Obligation are the days other than Sundays on which we celebrate the great things God has done for us through Jesus and the saints. On Holy Days of Obligation, Catholics gather for Mass.

Six Holy Days of Obligation are celebrated in the United States.

January 1—Mary, Mother of God

40 days after Easter—Ascension (In many U.S. dioceses, it is the seventh Sunday of Easter.)

August 15—Assumption of the Blessed Virgin Mary

November 1—All Saints

December 8—Immaculate Conception

December 25—Nativity of Our Lord Jesus Christ

Ascension.

Precepts of the Church

The Precepts of the Church describe the minimum effort we must make in prayer and in living a moral life. All Catholics are called to move beyond the minimum by growing in love of God and love of neighbor. The Precepts are as follows:

1. To keep holy the day of the Lord's Resurrection. To worship God by participating in Mass every Sunday and on Holy Days of Obligation. To avoid those activities (like needless work) that would hinder worship, joy, or relaxation.

2. To lead a sacramental life. To receive Holy Communion frequently and celebrate the Sacrament of Reconciliation regularly.

3. To study Catholic teaching in preparation for the Sacrament of Confirmation and to be confirmed, and then to continue to study and advance the cause of Christ.

4. To observe the marriage laws of the Church. To give religious training, by word and example, to one's children. To use parish schools and catechetical programs.

5. To strengthen and support the Church—one's own parish and parish priests, the worldwide Church, and the pope.

6. To do penance, including abstaining from meat and fasting from food on the appointed days.

7. To join in the missionary spirit and apostolate of the Church.

Living Our Faith

The Ten Commandments

As believers in Jesus Christ, we are called to a new life and are asked to make moral choices that keep us unified with God. With the help and grace of the Holy Spirit, we can choose ways to act that keep us close to God, help other people, and be witnesses to Jesus in the world.

The Ten Commandments guide us in making choices that help us live as God wants us to live. The first three commandments tell us how to love God; the other seven tell us how to love our neighbor.

Moses with the Ten Commandments.

1. I am the Lord your God: you shall not have strange gods before me.

2. You shall not take the name of the Lord your God in vain.

3. Remember to keep holy the Lord's Day.

4. Honor your father and your mother.

5. You shall not kill.

6. You shall not commit adultery.

7. You shall not steal.

8. You shall not bear false witness against your neighbor.

9. You shall not covet your neighbor's wife.

10. You shall not covet your neighbor's goods.

The Great Commandment

The Ten Commandments are fulfilled in Jesus' Great Commandment: "You shall love God with all your heart, with all your soul, with all your mind, and with all your strength.

You shall love your neighbor as yourself." (adapted from Mark 12:30–31)

The New Commandment

Before his death on the cross, Jesus gave his disciples a new commandment: "Love one another. As I have loved you, so you also should love one another." (John 13:34)

The Church of the Beatitudes, overlooking the Sea of Galilee, Israel.

The Beatitudes

The Beatitudes are the teachings of Jesus in the Sermon on the Mount, described in Matthew 5:1–10. The Beatitudes fulfill God's promises made to Abraham and to his descendants and describe the rewards that will be ours as loyal followers of Christ.

Blessed are the poor in spirit,
for theirs is the kingdom of heaven.

Blessed are they who mourn,
for they will be comforted.

Blessed are the meek,
for they will inherit the land.

Blessed are they who hunger and thirst
for righteousness,
for they will be satisfied.

Blessed are the merciful,
for they will be shown mercy.

Blessed are the clean of heart,
for they will see God.

Blessed are the peacemakers,
for they will be called children of God.

Blessed are they who are persecuted
for the sake of righteousness,
for theirs is the kingdom of heaven.

Making Good Choices

Our conscience is the inner voice that helps us know the law God has placed in our hearts. Our conscience helps us to judge the moral qualities of our own actions. It guides us to do good and avoid evil.

The Holy Spirit can help us form a good conscience. We form our conscience by studying the teachings of the Church and following the guidance of our parents and pastoral leaders.

God has given every human being freedom of choice. This does not mean that we have the right to do whatever we please. We can live in true freedom with the Holy Spirit, who gives us the virtue of prudence. This virtue helps us recognize what is good in every situation and to make correct choices. The Holy Spirit gives us the gifts of wisdom and understanding to help us make the right choices in life in relationship to God and others. The gift of counsel helps us reflect on making correct choices in life.

The Ten Commandments help us make

moral choices that are pleasing to God. We have the grace of the sacraments, the teachings of the Church, and the good example of saints and fellow Christians to help us make good choices.

Making moral choices involves the following steps:

1. Ask the Holy Spirit for help.

2. Think about God's law and the teachings of the Church.

3. Think about what will happen as a result of your choice.

4. Seek advice from someone you respect, and remember that Jesus is with you.

5. Ask yourself how your choice will affect your relationships with God and others.

Making moral choices takes into consideration the object of the choice, our intention in making the choice, and the circumstances in which the choice is made. It is never right to make an evil choice in the hope of gaining something good.

An Examination of Conscience

An examination of conscience is the act of reflecting on how we have hurt our relationships with God and others. The questions below help us in our examination of conscience.

My Relationship with God

What steps am I taking to help me grow closer to God and to others?

Do I participate at Mass with attention and devotion on Sundays and holy days?

Do I pray often and read the Bible?

Do I use God's name and the names of Jesus, Mary, and the saints with love and reverence?

My Relationships with Family, Friends, and Neighbors

Have I set a bad example by my words or actions? Have I treated others fairly? Have I spread stories that hurt other people?

Am I loving toward those in my family? Am I respectful of my neighbors, my friends, and those in authority?

Do I show respect for my body and for the bodies of others? Do I keep away from forms of entertainment that do not respect God's gift of sexuality?

Have I taken or damaged anything that did not belong to me? Have I cheated, copied homework, or lied?

Do I quarrel with others just so I can get my own way? Do I insult others to try to make them think they are less than I am? Do I hold grudges and try to hurt people who I think have hurt me?

How to Make a Good Confession

An examination of conscience is an important part of preparing for the Sacrament of Penance and Reconciliation. Reconciliation includes the following steps:

- The priest greets us, and we pray the Sign of the Cross. He invites us to trust in God. He may read God's Word with us.

- We confess our sins. The priest may help and counsel us.

- The priest gives us a penance to perform. Penance is an act of kindness or prayers to pray, or both.

- The priest asks us to express our sorrow, usually by reciting the Act of Contrition.

- We receive absolution. The priest says, "I absolve you from your sins in the name of the Father, and of the Son, and of the Holy Spirit." We respond, "Amen."

- The priest dismisses us by saying, "Go in peace." We go forth to perform the act of penance he has given us.

Virtues

Virtues are gifts from God that lead us to live in a close relationship with him. Virtues are like habits. They need to be practiced; they can be lost if they are neglected. The three most important virtues are called the *theological virtues* because they come from God and lead to God. The *cardinal virtues* are human virtues acquired by education and good actions. *Cardinal* comes from *cardo,* the Latin word for *hinge,* meaning "that on which other things depend."

Theological Virtues
faith   hope   charity

Cardinal Virtues
prudence   fortitude
justice   temperance

Gifts of the Holy Spirit

The Holy Spirit makes it possible for us to do what God asks by giving us these gifts.

wisdom   understanding
counsel   fortitude
knowledge   fear of the Lord
piety

Fruits of the Holy Spirit
The Fruits of the Holy Spirit are signs of the Holy Spirit's action in our lives.

love   joy   peace
patience   kindness   generosity
goodness   chastity   faithfulness
gentleness self-control modesty

Works of Mercy

The Corporal and Spiritual Works of Mercy are actions we can perform that extend God's compassion and mercy to those in need.

Corporal Works of Mercy

The Corporal Works of Mercy are the kind acts by which we help our neighbors with their material and physical needs:

Feed the hungry.

Shelter the homeless.

Clothe the naked.

Visit the sick and the imprisoned.

Give alms to the poor.

Bury the dead.

Spiritual Works of Mercy

The Spiritual Works of Mercy are acts of compassion by which we help our neighbors with their emotional and spiritual needs:

Instruct.

Advise.

Console.

Comfort.

Forgive.

Bear wrongs with patience.

The Bible and You

most important books of the New Testament are the four Gospels—Matthew, Mark, Luke, and John. Many of the 27 books are letters written by Saint Paul.

How Do You Find a Passage in the Bible?

Bible passages are identified by book, chapter, and verse—for example, Gn 1:28. The name of the book comes first. It is often abbreviated. Your Bible's table of contents will help you find out what the abbreviation means. In our example, *Gn* stands for the *Book of Genesis.* After the name of the book, there are two or more numbers. The first number identifies the chapter, which in our example is chapter 1. The chapter number is followed by a colon. The second number or numbers identify the verses. Our example shows verse 28.

God speaks to us in many ways. One way that God speaks to us is through the Bible. The Bible is the most important book in Christian life because it is God's message, or revelation. The Bible is the story of God's promise to care for us, especially through his Son, Jesus. At Mass we hear stories from the Bible. We can also read the Bible on our own.

The Bible is not just one book; it is a collection of many books. The writings in the Bible were inspired by the Holy Spirit and written by different authors using different styles.

The Bible is made up of two parts. The Old Testament contains 46 books that tell stories about the Jewish people and their faith in God before Jesus was born. It also contains the Ten Commandments, which guide us to live as God wants us to live.

The New Testament contains 27 books that tell the story of Jesus' life, death, and Resurrection, and the experience of the early Christians. For Christians the

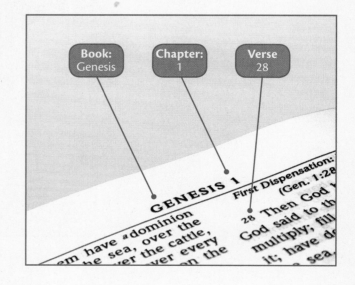

Showing Our Love for the World

Through the themes of Catholic Social Teaching, the Church encourages us to participate in the following areas of social action.

Life and Dignity of the Human Person

All human life is sacred, and all people must be respected and valued over material goods. We are called to ask whether our actions as a society respect or threaten the life and dignity of the human person.

Call to Family, Community, and Participation

Families must be supported so that people can participate in society, build a community spirit, and promote the well-being of all, especially the poor and vulnerable.

Rights and Responsibilities

Every person has a right to life as well as a right to those things required for human decency. As Catholics, we have a responsibility to protect these basic human rights in order to achieve a healthy society.

Option for the Poor and Vulnerable

In our world many people are rich, while others are extremely poor. As Catholics, we are called to pay special attention to the needs of the poor by defending and promoting their dignity and by meeting their immediate material needs.

The Dignity of Work and the Rights of Workers

The basic rights of workers must be respected: the right to productive work, fair wages, and private property; and the right to organize, join unions, and pursue economic opportunity. Catholics believe that the economy is meant to serve people and that work is not merely a way to make a living, but is an important way in which we participate in God's creation.

Solidarity

Because God is our Father, we are all brothers and sisters with the responsibility to care for one another. Solidarity is the attitude that leads Christians to share spiritual and material goods. Solidarity unites rich and poor, weak and strong, and helps create a society that recognizes that we depend on one another.

Care for God's Creation

God is the creator of all people and all things, and he wants us to enjoy his creation. The responsibility to care for all that God has made is a requirement of our faith.

Glossary

A

Abba an informal word for *Father* in the language Jesus spoke. Jesus called God the Father "Abba."

absolution the forgiveness God offers us in the Sacrament of Penance and Reconciliation. After we say that we are sorry for our sins, we receive God's absolution from the priest.

adore to worship God above all else because he is our creator. The First Commandment tells us to adore God.

adultery being unfaithful to one's marriage partner. A person who commits adultery breaks his or her marriage promises.

altar the table in the church on which the priest celebrates Mass, during which the sacrifice of Christ on the cross is made present in the Sacrament of the Eucharist. The altar represents two aspects of the mystery of the Eucharist. First, it is where Jesus Christ offers himself for our sins. Second, it is where he gives us himself as our food for eternal life.

ambo a raised stand from which a person reads the Word of God during Mass

angel a spiritual creature who brings a message from God

Angelus a prayer honoring the Incarnation of Jesus. The Angelus is prayed in the morning, at noon, and in the evening.

Annunciation the announcement to Mary by the angel Gabriel that God had chosen her to be the mother of Jesus

apostle one of twelve special men who accompanied Jesus in his ministry and were witnesses to the Resurrection

Apostles' Creed a statement of Christian belief. The Apostles' Creed, developed out of a creed used in Baptism in Rome, lists simple statements of belief in God the Father, Jesus Christ the Son, and the Holy Spirit. The profession of faith used in Baptism today is based on the Apostles' Creed.

Ascension the return of Jesus to heaven. In the Acts of the Apostles, it is written that Jesus, after his Resurrection, spent 40 days on earth, instructing his followers. He then returned to his Father in heaven.

Assumption Mary's being taken to heaven, body and soul, by God at the end of her life. The feast of the Assumption is celebrated on August 15.

B

Baptism the first of the three sacraments by which we become members of the Church. Baptism frees us from original sin and gives us new life in Jesus Christ through the Holy Spirit.

Beatitudes the eight ways we can behave to live a blessed life. Jesus teaches us that if we live according to the Beatitudes, we will live a happy Christian life.

benediction a prayer service in which we honor Jesus in the Blessed Sacrament and receive his blessing

Bible the collection of books that tell the history of God's promise to care for us and his call for us to be faithful to him. God asked that people be faithful first through the beliefs of the Jewish people and then through belief in the life, death, and Resurrection of Jesus Christ.

bishop a man who has received the fullness of Holy Orders. He has inherited his duties from the original apostles. He cares for the Church today and is a principal teacher in the Church.

Blessed Sacrament the bread that has been consecrated by the priest at Mass. It is kept in the tabernacle to adore and to be taken to the sick.

blessing a prayer that calls for God's power and care upon some person, place, thing, or special activity

Body and Blood of Christ the bread and wine that has been consecrated by the priest at Mass. It still looks like bread and wine, but it is actually the Body and Blood of Jesus Christ.

C

catholic one of the four Marks of the Church. The Church is catholic because Jesus is fully present in it and because Jesus has given the Church to the whole world.

charity a virtue given to us by God. Charity helps us love God above all things and our neighbor as ourselves.

Christ a title that means "anointed with oil." It is from a Greek word that means the same thing as the Hebrew word *Messiah,* or "anointed." It is the name given to Jesus after the Resurrection.

Christian the name given to all those who have been anointed through the gift of the Holy Spirit in Baptism and have become followers of Jesus Christ

Christmas the day on which we celebrate the birth of Jesus (December 25)

Church the name given to all the followers of Christ throughout the world. It is also the name of the building where we gather to pray to God and the name of our community as we gather to praise God.

commandment a standard, or rule, for living as God wants us to live. Jesus summarized all the commandments into two: love God and love your neighbor.

Communion of Saints the union of all who have been saved in Jesus Christ, both those who are alive and those who have died

confession the act of telling our sins to a priest in the Sacrament of Penance and Reconciliation. The sacrament itself is sometimes referred to as "confession."

Confirmation the sacrament that completes the grace we receive in Baptism. Confirmation seals, or confirms, this grace through the seven Gifts of the Holy Spirit that we receive as part of Confirmation. This sacrament also unites us more closely in Jesus Christ.

conscience the inner voice that helps each of us know the law that God has placed in our hearts. It guides us to do good and avoid evil.

contrition the sorrow we feel when we know that we have sinned, followed by the decision not to sin again. Contrition is the most important part of our celebration of the Sacrament of Penance and Reconciliation.

Corporal Works of Mercy kind acts by which we help our neighbors with their everyday, material needs. Corporal Works of Mercy include feeding the hungry, finding a home for the homeless, clothing the naked, visiting the sick and those in prison, giving alms to the poor, and burying the dead.

covenant a solemn agreement between people or between people and God. God made covenants with humanity through agreements with Noah, Abraham, and Moses. These covenants offered salvation. God's new and final covenant was established through Jesus' life, death, and Resurrection.

Creation God's act of making everything that exists outside himself. Creation is everything that exists. God said that all creation is good.

Creator God, who made everything that is and whom we can come to know through everything he created

creed a brief summary of what people believe. The Apostles' Creed is a summary of Christian beliefs.

D

deacon a man ordained through the Sacrament of Holy Orders to help the bishop and priests in the work of the Church

devil a spirit created good by God who became evil because of disobedience. The devil tempted Jesus in the desert.

disciple a person who has accepted Jesus' message and tries to live as he did

E

Easter the celebration of the bodily raising of Jesus Christ from the dead. Easter is the most important Christian feast.

Emmanuel a name from the Old Testament that means "God with us." Because Jesus is always with us, we often call him by the name *Emmanuel.*

epistle a letter written by Saint Paul or another leader to a group of Christians in the early Church. Twenty-one of the 27 books of the New Testament are epistles.

Eucharist the sacrament in which we give thanks to God for giving us Jesus Christ in the bread and wine that become the Body and Blood of Jesus. This sacrament brings us into union with Jesus and his saving death and Resurrection.

examination of conscience the act of prayerfully thinking about what we have said or done that may have hurt our relationship with God or others. An examination of conscience is an important part of preparing to celebrate the Sacrament of Penance and Reconciliation.

F

faith a gift of God that helps us believe in him and live as he wants us to live. We express our faith in the words of the Apostles' Creed.

fasting limiting the amount we eat for a period of time, to express sorrow for sin and to make ourselves more aware of God's action in our lives

free will our ability to choose to do good because God has made us like him

G

Gospel the good news of God's mercy and love. We experience this news in the story of Jesus' life, death, and Resurrection. The story is presented to us in four books in the New Testament: the Gospels of Matthew, Mark, Luke, and John.

grace the gift of God given to us without our deserving it. Sanctifying grace fills us with his life and enables us to always be his friends. Grace also helps us live as God wants us to.

Great Commandment Jesus' essential teaching that we are to love God and to love our neighbor as we love ourselves

H

heaven the life with God that is full of happiness and never ends

Hebrews the descendants of Abraham, Isaac, and Jacob, who were enslaved in Egypt. God helped Moses lead the Hebrew people out of slavery.

holy one of the four Marks of the Church. It is the kind of life we live when we share in the life of God, who is all holiness. The Church is holy because of its union with Jesus Christ.

Holy Communion the consecrated bread and wine that we receive at Mass, which is the Body and Blood of Jesus Christ. It brings us into union with Jesus Christ and his saving death and Resurrection.

Holy Family the family made up of Jesus; his mother, Mary; and his foster father, Joseph

Holy Spirit the third Person of the Trinity, who is sent to us as our helper and, through Baptism and Confirmation, fills us with God's life.

homily an explanation of God's Word. A homily explains the words of God that we hear in the Bible readings at church.

hope the trust that God will always be with us. We also trust that he will make us happy now and help us live in a way that keeps us with him forever.

I

Incarnation the Son of God, Jesus, being born as a full human being in order to save us. The Incarnation is one of the main mysteries of our faith.

inspired influenced by the Holy Spirit. The human authors of Scripture were influenced by the Holy Spirit. The creative inspiration of the Holy Spirit makes sure that the Scripture is taught according to the truth God wants us to know for our salvation.

Israelites the descendants of Abraham, Isaac, and Jacob. God changed Jacob's name to "Israel," and Jacob's 12 sons and their children became the leaders of the 12 tribes of Israel. (*See* Hebrews.)

J

Jesus the Son of God, who was born of the Virgin Mary and who died and was raised from the dead so that we can live with God forever. His name means "God saves."

Joseph the foster father of Jesus, who was engaged to Mary when the angel announced that Mary would have a child through the power of the Holy Spirit

justice the strong, firm desire to give to God and others what is due them. Justice is one of the four central human virtues, called the cardinal virtues, by which we guide our Christian life.

K

Kingdom of God God's rule over us. We experience the Kingdom of God in part now, and we will experience it fully in heaven. The Kingdom of God was announced in the Gospel and is present in the Eucharist.

L

Last Supper the last meal Jesus ate with his disciples on the night before he died. At the Last Supper, Jesus took bread and wine, blessed them, and said that they were his Body and Blood. Every Mass is a remembrance of this last meal.

Lectionary the book that contains all the Bible stories we read at Mass

Liturgy of the Eucharist the second half of the Mass, in which the bread and wine are blessed and become the Body and Blood of Jesus Christ. We then receive the Body and Blood of Jesus Christ in Holy Communion.

Liturgy of the Word the first half of the Mass, in which we listen to God's Word from the Bible and consider what it means for us today

Lord the name for God that was used in place of the name he revealed to Moses, *Yahweh,* which was considered too sacred to pronounce. The New Testament also uses the title Lord for Jesus, recognizing him as God himself.

Lord's Day Sunday is the day Christians set aside for special worship of God. Each Sunday mass commemorates the Resurrection of Jesus on Easter Sunday. Besides telling us to offer God worship we all owe him, the Third Commandment says Sunday is a day for relaxation of mind and body and to perform works of mercy.

M

martyrs those who have given their lives for the faith. It comes from the Greek word for "witness." A martyr is the supreme witness to the truth of the faith and to Christ to whom he or she is united. The seventh chapter of the Acts of the Apostles recounts the death of the first martyr, the deacon Stephen.

Mary the mother of Jesus. She is called blessed and "full of grace" because God chose her to be the mother of the Son of God.

Mass the most important sacramental celebration of the Church. The celebration of the Mass was established by Jesus at the Last Supper as a remembrance of his death and Resurrection. At Mass we listen to God's Word from the Bible and receive Jesus Christ in the bread and wine that has been blessed to become his Body and Blood.

Messiah a title that means "anointed with oil." It is from a Hebrew word that means the same as the Greek word *Christ,* the name given to Jesus after the Resurrection.

miracle an act of wonder that cannot be explained by natural causes but is a work of God. In the Gospels, Jesus works miracles as a sign that the Kingdom of God is present in his ministry.

mission the work of Jesus Christ that is continued in the Church through the Holy Spirit. The mission of the Church is to proclaim salvation through Jesus' life, death, and Resurrection.

moral choice a choice to do what is right. We make moral choices because they are what we believe God wants. We can make them because we have the freedom to choose what is right and avoid what is wrong.

moral law a rule for living that has been established by God and people in authority who are concerned about the good of all people. Moral laws are based on God's direction to us to do what is right and to avoid what is wrong.

mortal sin a serious decision to turn away from God by doing something that we know is wrong and so cuts us off from God's life

mystery a truth revealed by God that we cannot completely understand. The truth that the Son of God became man is a mystery of our faith.

N

New Testament the 27 books of the second part of the Bible, which tell of the teaching, ministry, and saving events of the life of Jesus. The four Gospels present Jesus' life, death, and Resurrection. The Acts of the Apostles tells the story of the message of salvation as it spreads through the growth of the Church. Various letters instruct us on how to live as followers of Jesus Christ. The Book of Revelation offers encouragement to Christians living through persecution.

O

obedience the act of willingly following what God asks us to do for our salvation. The Fourth Commandment requires children to obey their parents, and all people are required to obey civil authority when it acts for the good of all.

Old Testament the first 46 books of the Bible, which tell of God's covenant with the people of Israel and his plan for the salvation of all people. The first five books are known as the Torah. The Old Testament is fulfilled in the New Testament, but God's covenant presented in the Old Testament has permanent value and has never been revoked, or set aside.

Ordinary Time the part of the liturgical year outside of the seasons of feasts and the preparation for them. Ordinary means not common, but counted time, as in ordinal numbers. It is devoted to growth in understanding the mystery of Christ in its fullness. The color of Ordinary Time is green to symbolize growth.

original sin the result of the sin by which the first human beings disobeyed God and chose to follow their own will rather than God's will. Because of this act, all human beings lost the original blessing that God intended, and they became subject to sin and death. In Baptism we are restored to life with God through Jesus Christ.

P

parable one of the simple stories that Jesus told to show us what the Kingdom of God is like. Parables present images, or scenes, drawn from everyday life. These images show us the radical, or serious, choice we make when we respond to the invitation to enter the Kingdom of God.

parish a community of believers in Jesus Christ who meet regularly in a specific area to worship God under the leadership of a pastor

Paschal Mystery the work of salvation accomplished by Jesus Christ through his passion, death, Resurrection, and Ascension. The Paschal Mystery is celebrated in the liturgy of the Church. Its saving effects are experienced by us in the sacraments.

Passover the Jewish festival that commemorates the delivery of the Hebrew people from slavery in Egypt. In the Eucharist we celebrate our passover from death to life through Jesus' death and Resurrection.

penance the turning away from sin because we want to live as God wants us to live (*See* Sacrament of Penance and Reconciliation.)

Pentecost the 50th day after Jesus was raised from the dead. On this day the Holy Spirit was sent from heaven, and the Church was born.

personal sin a sin we choose to commit, whether serious (mortal) or less serious (venial). Although the result of original sin is to leave us with a tendency to sin, God's grace, especially through the sacraments, helps us choose good over sin.

pope the Bishop of Rome, successor of Saint Peter, and leader of the Roman Catholic Church. Because he has the authority to act in the name of Christ, the pope is called the Vicar of Christ. The pope and all the bishops together make up the living, teaching office of the Church.

prayer the raising of our hearts and minds to God. We are able to speak to and listen to God in prayer because he teaches us how to do so.

prayer of petition a request of God asking him to fulfill a need. When we share in God's saving love, we understand that every need is one that we can ask God to help us with through petition.

Precepts of the Church those positive requirements that the pastoral authority of the Church has determined as necessary. These requirements describe the minimum effort we must make in prayer and the moral life. The Precepts of the Church ensure that all Catholics move beyond the minimum by growing in love of God and love of neighbor.

priest a man who has accepted God's special call to serve the Church by guiding it and building it up through the celebration of the sacraments

prophet a person called by God to speak to the people for him. John the Baptist was a great prophet.

psalm a prayer in the form of a poem. Psalms were written to be sung in public worship. Each psalm expresses an aspect, or feature, of the depth of human prayer. Over several centuries 150 psalms were gathered to form the Book of Psalms, used in worship in Old Testament times.

purgatory a state of final cleansing after death of all our human imperfections to prepare us to enter into the joy of God's presence in heaven

R

reconciliation the renewal of friendship after that friendship has been broken by some action or lack of action. In the Sacrament of Penance and Reconciliation, through God's mercy and forgiveness, we are reconciled with God, the Church, and others.

Redeemer Jesus Christ, whose life, death on the cross, and Resurrection from the dead set us free from sin and bring us redemption.

Resurrection the bodily raising of Jesus Christ from the dead on the third day after his death on the cross. The Resurrection is the crowning truth of our faith.

Revelation God's communication of himself to us through the words and deeds he has used throughout history. Revelation shows us the mystery of his plan for our salvation in his Son, Jesus Christ.

Rosary a prayer in honor of the Blessed Virgin Mary. When we pray the Rosary, we meditate on the mysteries of Jesus Christ's life while praying the Hail Mary on five sets of 10 beads and the Lord's Prayer on the beads in between.

S

Sabbath the seventh day, when God rested after finishing the work of creation. The Third Commandment requires us to keep the Sabbath holy. For Christians Sunday became the Sabbath because it was the day Jesus rose from the dead and the new creation in Jesus Christ began.

sacrament one of seven ways through which God's life enters our lives through the work of the Holy Spirit. Jesus gave us three sacraments that bring us into the Church: Baptism, Confirmation, and the Eucharist. He gave us two sacraments that bring us healing: Penance and Anointing of the Sick. He also gave us two sacraments that help members serve the community: Matrimony and Holy Orders.

Sacrament of Penance and Reconciliation the sacrament in which we celebrate God's forgiveness of our sins and our reconciliation with God and the Church. Reconciliation includes sorrow for the sins we have committed, confession of sins, absolution by the priest, and doing the penance that shows our sorrow.

sacramental an object, a prayer, or a blessing given by the Church to help us grow in our spiritual life

sacrifice a gift given to God to give him thanks. Jesus' sacrifice on the cross was the greatest sacrifice.

Sacrifice of the Mass the sacrifice of Jesus on the cross, which is remembered and made present in the Eucharist

saint a holy person who has died and is united with God. The Church has said that this person is now with God forever in heaven.

salvation the gift of forgiveness of sin and the restoration of friendship with God. God alone can give us salvation.

Satan the leader of the evil spirits. His name means "adversary." God allows Satan to tempt us.

Savior Jesus, the Son of God, who became human to forgive our sins and restore our friendship with God. *Jesus* means "God saves."

Scripture the holy writings of Jews and Christians collected in the Old and New Testaments of the Bible

Sermon on the Mount the words of Jesus, written in chapters 5 through 7 of the Gospel of Matthew, in which Jesus reveals how he has fulfilled God's law given to Moses. The Sermon on the Mount begins with the eight Beatitudes and includes the Lord's Prayer.

sin a choice we make on purpose that offends God and hurts our relationships with other people. Some sin is mortal and needs to be confessed in the Sacrament of Penance and Reconciliation. Other sin is venial, or less serious.

Son of God the title revealed by Jesus that indicates his unique relationship to God the Father

soul the part of us that makes us human and an image of God. Body and soul together form one unique human nature. The soul is responsible for our consciousness and our freedom.

Spiritual Works of Mercy the kind acts through which we help our neighbors meet the needs that are more than material. The Spiritual Works of Mercy include instructing, advising, consoling, comforting, forgiving, and bearing wrongs with patience.

synagogue the Jewish place of assembly for prayer, instruction, and study of the Law. Jesus attended the synagogue regularly to pray and to teach.

T

tabernacle a container in which the Blessed Sacrament is kept so that Holy Communion can be taken to the sick and the dying.

Temple the center of Jewish worship in Jerusalem where sacrifices were offered to God

temptation an attraction, from outside us or from inside us, that can lead us to not follow God's commands

Ten Commandments the 10 rules that God gave to Moses on Mount Sinai that sum up God's law and show us what is required to love God and our neighbor

Trinity the mystery of one God existing in three Persons: the Father, the Son, and the Holy Spirit.

V

venial sin a choice we make that weakens our relationship with God or other people. It wounds and diminishes the divine life in us.

W

witness the passing on to others, by our words and actions, the faith that we have been given. Every Christian has the duty to give witness to the good news about Jesus Christ that he or she has come to know.

worship the adoration and honor given to God in public prayer

Y

Yahweh the name of God in Hebrew, which God told Moses from the burning bush. *Yahweh* means "I am who am." Out of respect for God's name, Jews never say this name but replace it with other names.

Index

A

Abba, 126, 219
Abraham
  faith, 5
  God calls, 5, 33, 75
  God's promises to, 40–41
Abram, 5
absolution, 219
Act of Contrition, 156
acts of mercy. *See*
  merciful acts
Adam and Eve, 70, 71, 141
adore, 219
adultery, 219
Advent, 185
All Saints Day, 183, 184
All Souls Day, 184
alleluia, 193
almsgiving, 190
altar, 219
ambo, 219
Ananais, 29
Andrew, Saint, 27
angel, 219
Angelus, The, 201, 219
Anna, 77
Annunciation, 21, 22, 26, 33, 34b, 75, 219
anointing, 154
Anointing of the Sick, 207
apostles. *See also* disciples
  Creed (*see* Apostles' Creed)
  definition, 30, 219
  Jesus calls, 27
Apostles' Creed, 37, 219
Ascension, 117, 193, 219
Ash Wednesday, 189
Assumption, 131, 219
Ave Maria, 202. *See also*
  Hail Mary

B

Baptism, 207
  celebration of new life
    in God, 143, 144
  definition, 219
  faith, gift of, 5, 7
  grace, gift of, 144
  Holy Spirit's presence, 125
  Jesus' teachings
    regarding, 142
  water, 180a
Beatitudes, 212, 219
Benedict XVI, Pope, 202
benediction, 166, 219
Bethlehem, 76
Bible, 4, 216, 219
bishop, 219
Blessed Sacrament, 18, 219.
  See also Eucharist
blessing, 166, 219

Body and Blood of Christ

Body and Blood of Christ, 47, 104, 165, 172, 219.
  See also Eucharist;
  Holy Communion
Boaz, 6
burning bush, 41, 51

C

Calvary, 106
Cana, miracle at wedding, 34c, 127
Canaan, 40
catholic, 219
Catholicism
  strengthening in families, 138b–38c
celebrations
  Celebrating Our Life with
    Jesus, 179–80
  Come, Lord Jesus, 137–38
  Greatness and Goodness
    of God, The, 65–66
  We Are God's Holy People,
    33–34
  We Pray for the
    Coming of God's
    Kingdom, 99–100
charity, 70, 214, 219
choices, good, 212–13
Chosen People, 104
Christ, 219. *See also*
  Jesus; Messiah
Christians
  definition, 219
  service to God, 85
Christmas, 220
  Jesus' birth, 75, 76
  play, 187–88
Church, 220
  family, as, 4
  social teachings, 217–18
Clare of Assisi, Saint, 18, 19, 33
commandment,
  definition, 220
Commandment, Great, 211, 221
Commandment, New, 211
Commandments, Ten, 48, 211, 224
  Fourth Commandment, 78
  Second Commandment, 52
Communion of Saints, 130, 183, 219
Confirmation, 207, 219
confession, 162, 220. *See also*
  Penance and
  Reconciliation,
  Sacrament of
conscience, 156, 220
contrition, 220
Contrition, Act of. *See* Act
  of Contrition

Corporal Works of Mercy

Corporal Works of Mercy, 220
covenant, 220
creation, 39, 54, 69, 220
Creator, 39, 220
creed, 37, 220 *See also*
  Apostles' Creed;
  Nicene Creed
Crucifixion, 106

D

Damascus, 28, 29
Daughters of Charity, 61
David, King, 75, 185
  crowning, 12
  God calls, 33
  protector, as, 11
  psalm writer, 12
  Ruth, relative of, 6
  shepherd, 11
  talents, uses, 11
deacon, 220
death, 114
devil, 71, 220
disciples, 220. *See also*
  apostles
  definition, 30
  Jesus calls, 28
  risen Christ, see the, 110
Dominic Savio, Saint, 152

E

Easter, 112, 193, 220
Elizabeth, 127
Elizabeth Ann Seton, Saint, 56
Emmanuel, 220
enemies, love for one's, 94
epistles, 168, 220
eternal life, 107, 147
Eucharist, 165, 166, 191, 220.
  See also Holy
  Communion
  gift of love, 171
  sacrament, 207
Eucharistic Prayer, 172
Eve, 70, 71, 141
examination of conscience, 156, 213, 220

F

faith, 5, 6, 7, 8, 70, 214, 220
fasting, 190, 220
Fatima, 23
fear, facing, 109
forgiveness
  God's, 59
  Jesus forgives many, 154–55
  parable of, 159–60

Penance and Reconciliation

Penance and
  Reconciliation (*see*
  Penance and Reconciliation,
  Sacrament of)
  sins, of, 153
Francis of Assisi, Saint, 17, 18, 19, 33, 111
free will, 220

G

Gabriel, 21, 22. *See also*
  Annunciation
garden of Gethsemane 105, 106
Gloria Patri, 202. *See also*
  Glory Be to the Father
Glorious Mysteries, 24, 205.
  See also Rosary
Glory Be to the Father, 24, 202, 203
God
  almighty, 63
  calls us, 19
  cares for us, 63
  covenant of love, 48–50
  creation, 39, 54, 69, 220
  Creator, 39, 220
  feeds us, 47
  forgiveness (*see* forgiveness)
  goodness, 39
  holy name, 52
  just, is, 59, 60, 63
  knows all, 54, 63
  life-giver, 70
  merciful, as, 59, 63
  messengers of, 22
  power of, 46
  presence of, 53, 54
  promises of, 40–41, 42, 63
Goliath, 11
Good Friday, 191–92
Good Shepherd, 60.
  See also Jesus
Gospels, 83, 168, 220
grace, 53, 70, 74, 84, 141, 142, 144, 221
Great Commandment, 181, 211, 220

H

Hail Mary, 24, 25, 202
Hail, Holy Queen, 200
"Hail, Holy Queen,
  Enthroned Above," 131
heaven, 113, 129, 143, 220
Hebrews, 40, 220
helping others, 94
Herod, 34b
holy, 15, 220
Holy Communion. *See*
  also Eucharist
  definition, 220
  uniting us with Jesus, 47
Holy Days of Obligation, 209

Scripture Index

Art Credits

When there is more than one picture on a page, credits are supplied in sequence, left to right, top to bottom. Page positions are abbreviated as follows: (t) top, (c) center, (b) bottom, (l) left, (r) right.

FRONTMATTER:
v(t) © The Crosiers/Gene Plaisted OSC
vi(b) © The Crosiers/Gene Plaisted OSC

UNIT 1:
3(t) © The Crosiers/Gene Plaisted OSC
4(t) Phil Martin Photography
5(b) Phil Martin Photography
5(t) Don Dyen
6 Don Dyen
9(b) © The Crosiers/Gene Plaisted OSC
11(b) Don Dyen
12(t) Don Dyen
12(b) Don Dyen
13(b) © The Crosiers/Gene Plaisted OSC
15(c) © The Crosiers/Gene Plaisted OSC
16 Len Ebert/PC&F Inc.
17(l) © The Crosiers/Gene Plaisted OSC
17(r) Don Dyen
18(t) © The Crosiers/Gene Plaisted OSC
21(t) © The Crosiers/Gene Plaisted OSC
22(b) W. P. Wittman Limited
23(b) © The Crosiers/Gene Plaisted OSC
25(br) © The Crosiers/Gene Plaisted OSC
27(b) Sally Schaedler
28(r) © The Crosiers/Gene Plaisted OSC
28(tl) W. P. Wittman Limited
28(bl) W. P. Wittman Limited
29 Kathryn Seckman Kirsch
31(t) Carol Tornatore
31(b) Kathryn Seckman Kirsch
32(t) © The Crosiers/Gene Plaisted OSC
32(bl) Laser Type & Graphics
32(br) Sally Schaedler
34a(b) W. P. Wittman Limited
34b(l) © The Crosiers/Gene Plaisted OSC
34b(b) Kathryn Seckman Kirsch
34c(t) © The Crosiers/Gene Plaisted OSC
34d Kathryn Seckman Kirsch

UNIT 2:
37(t) W. P. Wittman Limited
38(t) © The Crosiers/Gene Plaisted OSC
39(bc) Joseph Van Os/Riser/Getty Images
40 Don Dyen
41 Don Dyen
43 © Bettmann/Corbis
45(t) © The Crosiers/Gene Plaisted OSC
45(b) Don Dyen
46 Don Dyen
47(t) Phil Martin Photography
47(b) Don Dyen

48 Don Dyen
49(tl) Myrleen Ferguson/PhotoEdit
50 © The Crosiers/Gene Plaisted OSC
51(t) Peter Adams/The Image Bank/ Getty Images
51(b) Don Dyen
52 © The Crosiers/Gene Plaisted OSC
54(t) © The Crosiers/Gene Plaisted OSC
55(b) © The Crosiers/Gene Plaisted OSC
56 © The Crosiers/Gene Plaisted OSC
57(bl) © The Crosiers/Gene Plaisted OSC
57(cr) W. P. Wittman Limited
59 Myrleen Ferguson/PhotoEdit
60 © Lebrecht Music and Arts Photo Library/Alamy
61(tl) © The Crosiers/Gene Plaisted OSC
61(bl) © The Crosiers/Gene Plaisted OSC
62 © The Crosiers/Gene Plaisted OSC
64 Kathryn Seckman Kirsch
66b(b) Phil Martin Photography
66c(br) © Bettmann/Corbis
66c(tr) Phil Martin Photography
66c(bl) W. P. Wittman Limited
66d W. P. Wittman Limited

UNIT 3:
69(t) Grant Faint/Photographer's Choice/ Getty Images
70 Kathryn Seckman Kirsch
71 © The Crosiers/Gene Plaisted OSC
72 © The Crosiers/Gene Plaisted OSC
77(b) © The Crosiers/Gene Plaisted OSC
79(b) © The Crosiers/Gene Plaisted OSC
81(t) Phil Martin Photography
81(b) Sally Schaedler
83 Sally Schaedler
84(t) © The Crosiers/Gene Plaisted OSC
84(b) © The Crosiers/Gene Plaisted OSC
87(b) Sally Schaedler
88 Phyllis Pollema-Cahill
89 © The Crosiers/Gene Plaisted OSC
90(t) © The Crosiers/Gene Plaisted OSC
91(t) © The Crosiers/Gene Plaisted OSC
92 © The Crosiers/Gene Plaisted OSC
93(b) Sally Schaedler
94(r) Phil Martin Photography
97 © The Crosiers/Gene Plaisted OSC
100(r) Laser Type & Graphics
100c Kevin Peschke and Kathryn Seckman Kirsch

UNIT 4:
101 © The Crosiers/Gene Plaisted OSC
102 © The Crosiers/Gene Plaisted OSC
103(t) W. P. Wittman
103(b) Sally Schaedler
104 Sally Schaedler
105 © The Crosiers/Gene Plaisted OSC

106(t) Sally Schaedler
106(c) Sally Schaedler
108 Diana Bush
109(t) © The Crosiers/Gene Plaisted OSC
110 Sally Schaedler
111(b) © The Crosiers/Gene Plaisted OSC
112(br) © Jim West/Alamy
113 Phil Martin Photography
114(t) Hexx/Veer
115 © The Crosiers/Gene Plaisted OSC
117(b) Sally Schaedler
118(b) © The Crosiers/Gene Plaisted OSC
118(t) Myrleen Ferguson/PhotoEdit
119(b) Diana Bush
120(r) Phil Martin Photography
122 W. P. Wittman Limited
123(t) © The Crosiers/Gene Plaisted OSC
123(b) Betty Maxey
124(t) © The Crosiers/Gene Plaisted OSC
124(b) W. P. Wittman Limited
125(t) © The Crosiers/Gene Plaisted OSC
126 Kathryn Seckman Kirsch
127 © The Crosiers/Gene Plaisted OSC
128 © The Crosiers/Gene Plaisted OSC
129 Phil Martin Photography
131(t) © The Crosiers/Gene Plaisted OSC
131(b) © The Crosiers/Gene Plaisted OSC
132(b) © The Crosiers/Gene Plaisted OSC
133(tr) W. P. Wittman Limited
134 Elizabeth Wang, "The Glory and the Gathering," © Radiant Light 2006, www.radiantlight.org.uk
136(t) © The Crosiers/Gene Plaisted OSC
136(b) Kathryn Seckman Kirsch

UNIT 5:
141(b) Jim Cummins
142(t) Sally Schaedler
144(c) Laser Type & Graphics
145(t) © The Crosiers/Gene Plaisted OSC
145(bc) © The Crosiers/Gene Plaisted OSC
145(bl) Phil Martin Photography
147(c) Sally Schaedler
149(t) W. P. Wittman Limited
149(b) © The Crosiers/Gene Plaisted OSC
150 Carol Tornatore
151(l) © Cleo Freelance Photography
151(c) Phil Martin Photography
151(r) Phil Martin Photography
152(r) © The Crosiers/Gene Plaisted OSC
152(l) Fr. William Hart McNichols, http://puffin.creighton.edu/jesuit/andre
153(b) Sally Schaedler
154(l) Jim Cummins
154(r) Jim Cummins
155 Jim Cummins
156(b) © The Crosiers/Gene Plaisted OSC
157 Kathryn Seckman Kirsch

159(c) Jim Cummins
159(b) Jim Cummins
160(t) Jim Cummins
162 Phil Martin Photography
163 Diane Johnson and Kathryn Seckman Kirsch
164 Diana Bush and Kathryn Seckman Kirsch
165 © The Crosiers/Gene Plaisted OSC
166(t) © The Crosiers/Gene Plaisted OSC
167(t) Phyllis Pollema-Cahill
167(b) Phyllis Pollema-Cahill
168 W. P. Wittman Limited
169 Kathryn Seckman Kirsch
171(t) Stephen Smith/Photonica/Getty Images
171(b) © The Crosiers/Gene Plaisted OSC
172 W. P. Wittman Limited
173 Phyllis Pollema-Cahill
174(t) W. P. Wittman Limited
174(bl) W. P. Wittman Limited
175 Kathryn Seckman Kirsch
176(t) Robert Voigts
176(b) Jose Luis Pelaez Inc./Blend Images/Getty Images
177(t) © The Crosiers/Gene Plaisted OSC
180a(t) Phil Martin Photography
180a(br) Phil Martin Photography
180a(bc) W. P. Wittman Limited
180c(b) Phil Martin Photography

SPECIAL SEASONS AND LESSONS:
182 Susan Tolonen
185(t) © The Crosiers/Gene Plaisted OSC
186 Arist Kirsch
195 © The Crosiers/Gene Plaisted OSC
196(t) W. P. Wittman Limited

WHAT CATHOLICS SHOULD KNOW:
198(b) Myrleen Ferguson Cate/PhotoEdit
199(b) Lon C. Diehl/PhotoEdit
202(t) vario images GmbH & Co.KG/Alamy
202(b) Myrleen Ferguson Cate/PhotoEdit
203(t) © The Crosiers/Gene Plaisted OSC
204 Greg Kuepfer
205(t) CSI Productions/Alamy
206 From Fourteen Mosaic Stations of the Cross © Our Lady of the Angels Monastery Inc., Hanceville Alabama. All Rights Reserved
207(b) Greg Kuepfer
209(t) Myrleen Ferguson Cate/PhotoEdit
209(b) © The Crosiers/Gene Plaisted OSC
210(cr) Myrleen Ferguson Cate/PhotoEdit
211 Stock Montage, Inc./Alamy
212(t) © Richard T. Nowitz/Corbis
212(b) © The Crosiers/Gene Plaisted OSC
214 Myrleen Ferguson Cate/PhotoEdit
215(b) Myrleen Ferguson Cate/PhotoEdit
217 Jeff Greenberg/PhotoEdit

LESSON PULLOUTS:
229(t) Diana Bush
229(br) © The Crosiers/Gene Plaisted OSC
Reconciliation Booklet, cover:
© The Crosiers/Gene Plaisted OSC
Joyful Mysteries Booklet, 6: © The Crosiers/Gene Plaisted OSC
Joyful Mysteries Booklet, 8: Robert Korta
Joyful Mysteries Booklet, 4: © The Crosiers/Gene Plaisted OSC
Joyful Mysteries Booklet, 5: Robert Korta
Joyful Mysteries Booklet, 7: Robert Korta
Luminous Mysteries Booklet, 6 and 3:
© The Crosiers/Gene Plaisted OSC
Luminous Mysteries Booklet, 4:
© The Crosiers/Gene Plaisted OSC
Luminous Mysteries Booklet, 5 and 7:
Sally Schaedler

Sorrowful Mysteries Booklet, 6:
© The Crosiers/Gene Plaisted OSC
Sorrowful Mysteries Booklet, 8:
Robert Korta
Sorrowful Mysteries Booklet, 4:
© The Crosiers/Gene Plaisted OSC
Sorrowful Mysteries Booklet, 5 and 7:
Robert Korta
Glorious Mysteries Booklet, 6 and 3:
© The Crosiers/Gene Plaisted OSC
Glorious Mysteries Booklet, 4:
© The Crosiers/Gene Plaisted OSC
Glorious Mysteries Booklet, 5 and 7:
Robert Korta
Gifted with Faith Booklet, cover:
© The Crosiers/Gene Plaisted OSC
Gifted with Faith Booklet, 12:
Laser Type & Graphics
Gifted with Faith Booklet, 8: Diana Bush
Gifted with Faith Booklet, 6 and 7:
Bill Gorman
Palestine Map: Bill Wood
Old Testament Map: Bill Wood
Portrait of Jesus (perforated): Bill Gorman
Jesus with Children (perforated):
© The Crosiers/Gene Plaisted OSC
Tablets (perforated):
Kathryn Seckman Kirsch
Heart (perforated) and Instruction Art:
Bill Wise and Kathryn Seckman Kirsch

Lesson Pullouts

- **Reconciliation Booklet**
- **The Joyful Mysteries**
- **The Luminous Mysteries**
- **The Sorrowful Mysteries**
- **The Glorious Mysteries**
- **Gifted with Faith**
- **Map of Palestine in the Time of Jesus**
- **The Lands of the Old Testament Map**
- **Punch-outs**

Third Joyful Mystery

The Birth of Christ

The Son of God becomes the child Jesus. Mary is holding him in her arms. Saint Joseph is standing nearby, watching over them. See how much Mary and Joseph love the child Jesus!

Let us ask Mary to help us grow in love for Jesus.

6

Apostles' Creed

I believe in God, the Father almighty,
    creator of heaven and earth.
I believe in Jesus Christ, his only Son, our Lord.
    He was conceived by the power of the
        Holy Spirit
      and born of the Virgin Mary.
    He suffered under Pontius Pilate,
      was crucified, died, and was buried.
    He descended to the dead.
    On the third day he arose again.
    He ascended into heaven,
      and is seated at the right hand of
        the Father.
    He will come again to judge the living
      and the dead.
I believe in the Holy Spirit,
    the holy catholic Church,
    the communion of saints,
    the forgiveness of sins,
    the resurrection of the body,
    and the life everlasting. Amen.

3

Fifth Joyful Mystery

The Finding of Jesus

Jesus is missing for three days. How happy Mary and Joseph are to find him in the Temple. Jesus goes home with them and obeys them.

Let us ask Mary to teach us how to obey as Jesus did.

8

The Joyful Mysteries

My Rosary Book

First Joyful Mystery

The Annunciation

Mary is listening as the angel Gabriel speaks to her. He tells Mary that God has chosen her to be the Mother of his Son. Mary says, "Yes, I will do as God wills."

Let us ask Mary to help us say yes to all that God asks.

4

Second Joyful Mystery

The Visitation

See how happy Mary and Elizabeth are! Mary has come to help her relative Elizabeth. Elizabeth is honored to have Mary, the Mother of the Savior, visit her.

Let us ask Mary to help us be kind to others.

5

How to Pray the Rosary

1. Hold the crucifix and make the Sign of the Cross.
2. Say the Apostles' Creed while holding the cross.
3. On the first bead, say the Our Father.
4. On each of the three beads, say a Hail Mary for more faith, hope, and love.
5. Say the Glory Be to the Father on the chain before the large bead.
6. Call to mind the first mystery and think about it. Say the Our Father on the first bead.
7. On each of the 10 beads, say a Hail Mary. Keep the mystery in your mind.
8. After each set of 10 Hail Marys, say the Glory Be to the Father.
9. Say each decade the same way, thinking about each mystery.
10. Conclude by blessing yourself with the Sign of the Cross.

2

Fourth Joyful Mystery

The Presentation

Simeon comes to the Temple to pray every day. He tells God how happy he is to see the child Jesus. He says that Jesus will be a light for everyone.

Let us ask Mary to teach us how to pray.

7

Fourth Luminous Mystery

The Transfiguration

Jesus and his disciples Peter, James, and John climb a mountain. There the disciples see Jesus' face shine like the sun. They hear God the Father tell them to listen to his chosen Son.

Let us tell Jesus that we will listen to him and follow his example.

6

First Luminous Mystery

The Baptism of Jesus

Jesus goes to the Jordan River and is baptized by John the Baptist. As Jesus comes out of the water, the Holy Spirit comes to him in the form of a dove. The Father tells everyone that Jesus is his beloved Son.

Let us ask the Holy Spirit to help us tell everyone about Jesus.

3

Apostles' Creed

I believe in God, the Father almighty,
  creator of heaven and earth.
I believe in Jesus Christ, his only Son, our Lord.
    He was conceived by the power of the
        Holy Spirit
      and born of the Virgin Mary.
    He suffered under Pontius Pilate,
      was crucified, died, and was buried.
    He descended to the dead.
    On the third day he arose again.
    He ascended into heaven,
      and is seated at the right hand of
        the Father.
    He will come again to judge the living
      and the dead.
I believe in the Holy Spirit,
    the holy catholic Church,
    the communion of saints,
    the forgiveness of sins,
    the resurrection of the body,
    and the life everlasting. Amen.

8

The Luminous Mysteries

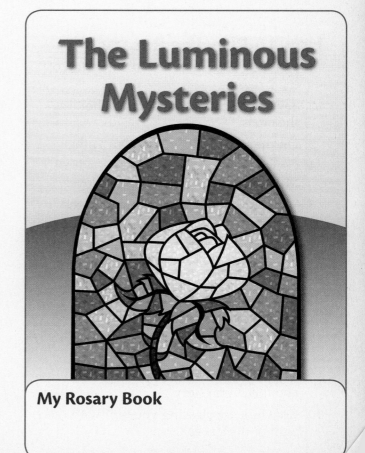

My Rosary Book

Second Luminous Mystery

The Wedding at Cana

Jesus goes to a wedding feast with Mary, his Mother. There he changes water into wine. Jesus' disciples see the miracle and believe in him.

Let us tell Jesus how happy we are that we believe in him too.

4

Third Luminous Mystery

Proclamation of the Kingdom

Jesus calls everyone to be close to him. Through his preaching and his life, Jesus teaches us how to serve the Kingdom of God.

Let us thank Jesus for showing us how to love him and others.

5

How to Pray the Rosary

1. Hold the crucifix and make the Sign of the Cross.
2. Say the Apostles' Creed while holding the cross.
3. On the first bead, say the Our Father.
4. On each of the three beads, say a Hail Mary for more faith, hope, and love.
5. Say the Glory Be to the Father on the chain before the large bead.
6. Call to mind the first mystery and think about it. Say the Our Father on the first bead.
7. On each of the 10 beads, say a Hail Mary. Keep the mystery in your mind.
8. After each set of 10 Hail Marys, say the Glory Be to the Father.
9. Say each decade the same way, thinking about each mystery.
10. Conclude by blessing yourself with the Sign of the Cross.

2

Fifth Luminous Mystery

The Institution of the Eucharist

While Jesus is at supper with his friends, he talks with them and shares bread and wine with them. Jesus offers them the gift of himself—his own Body and Blood—for their salvation and for ours.

Let us thank Jesus for saving us and tell him how much we love him.

7

Third Sorrowful Mystery

The Crowning with Thorns

After the scourging, the soldiers make fun of Jesus. They put a purple robe on him and crown him with thorns. They mock him by saying "Hail, King of the Jews!" Jesus does not say a word.

Let us ask Jesus to help us be kind to those who hurt us.

6

Apostles' Creed

I believe in God, the Father almighty,
     creator of heaven and earth.
I believe in Jesus Christ, his only Son, our Lord.
     He was conceived by the power of the
          Holy Spirit
          and born of the Virgin Mary.
     He suffered under Pontius Pilate,
          was crucified, died, and was buried.
     He descended to the dead.
     On the third day he arose again.
     He ascended into heaven,
          and is seated at the right hand of
               the Father.
     He will come again to judge the living
          and the dead.
I believe in the Holy Spirit,
     the holy catholic Church,
     the communion of saints,
     the forgiveness of sins,
     the resurrection of the body,
     and the life everlasting. Amen.

3

Fifth Sorrowful Mystery

The Death of Our Lord

Jesus suffers on the cross. He forgives his enemies and gives us Mary to be our Mother. He gives up his life so that we can live with him forever.

Let us thank Jesus for his great love and promise to show more love for him.

8

The Sorrowful Mysteries

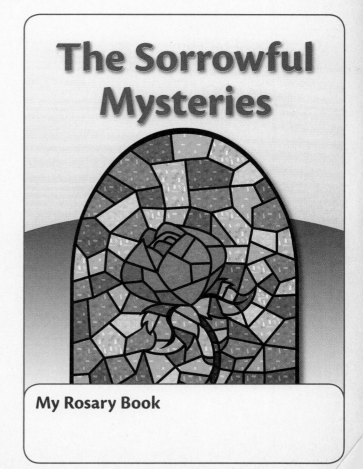

My Rosary Book

First Sorrowful Mystery

The Agony in the Garden

After the Last Supper, Jesus goes to the garden to pray. Peter, James, and John go with him. As Jesus thinks of his suffering to come, his sweat is like drops of blood. He offers his sufferings for our sins.

Let us tell Jesus how sorry we are for our sins.

4

Second Sorrowful Mystery

The Scourging

Because Pilate is afraid of the people, he has Jesus scourged, or whipped. The soldiers whip Jesus with heavy cords. Jesus suffers this for our sins.

Let us ask Jesus for mercy and forgiveness of our sins.

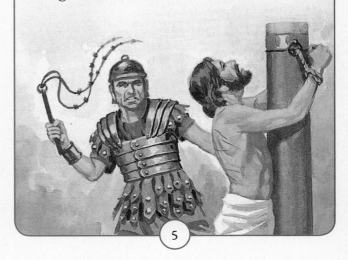

5

Color a bead each time you say your prayers.

2

Fourth Sorrowful Mystery

The Carrying of the Cross

Jesus carries the heavy cross because he loves us. How sad it is when he meets his Mother on the way! Jesus is so weak that he falls three times.

Let us ask Jesus to help us be brave when we have something difficult to do.

7

Fourth Glorious Mystery

The Assumption

After Jesus' death, Mary helps the apostles. When her life on earth ends, Jesus takes her, body and soul, into heaven. He does this because he truly loves his Mother and because she has never sinned.

Let us ask Mary to help us so that we may one day share in her glory.

6

First Glorious Mystery

The Resurrection

Jesus rises from the dead on the third day. He is seen by his Mother, by Mary Magdalene, and by the apostles. To the apostle Thomas, he says, "Blessed are those who have not seen and have believed."

Let us tell Jesus that we believe in him.

3

Color a bead each time you say your prayers.

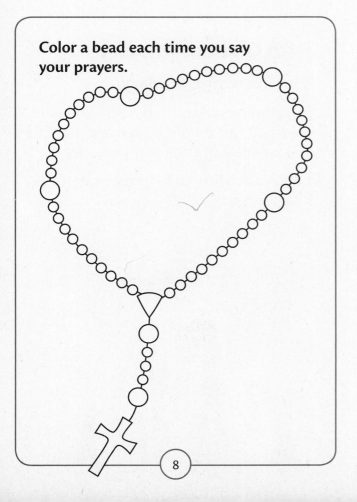

8

The Glorious Mysteries

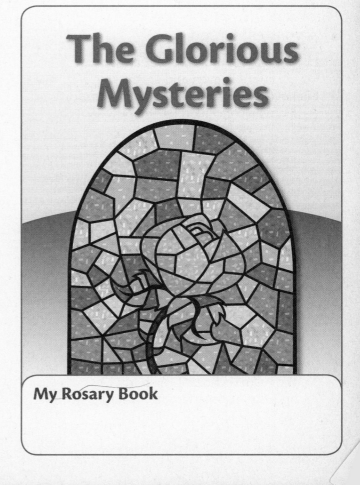

My Rosary Book

Second Glorious Mystery

The Ascension

Before Jesus ascends into heaven, he tells his apostles to teach the Good News and baptize people everywhere. He tells them to wait for the Holy Spirit. Then he ascends into heaven to prepare a place for everyone.

Let us tell Jesus that we hope to live with him in heaven some day.

Third Glorious Mystery

The Coming of the Holy Spirit

Mary and the other disciples wait and pray for the Holy Spirit to come. When he comes, tongues of fire can be seen above the head of each of the disciples. The Spirit fills their hearts with great love and courage.

Let us ask the Holy Spirit to make our love stronger.

Apostles' Creed

I believe in God, the Father almighty,
    creator of heaven and earth.
I believe in Jesus Christ, his only Son, our Lord.
    He was conceived by the power of the
        Holy Spirit
        and born of the Virgin Mary.
    He suffered under Pontius Pilate,
        was crucified, died, and was buried.
    He descended to the dead.
    On the third day he arose again.
    He ascended into heaven,
        and is seated at the right hand of
        the Father.
    He will come again to judge the living
        and the dead.
I believe in the Holy Spirit,
    the holy catholic Church,
    the communion of saints,
    the forgiveness of sins,
    the resurrection of the body,
    and the life everlasting. Amen.

Fifth Glorious Mystery

The Crowning of Mary

Jesus honors Mary in heaven. She is crowned Queen of Heaven and Earth. She watches over us and prays for us.

Let us ask Mary to help us grow in love for Jesus.

Think and pray about each of these ways that we show we belong to the Kingdom of God.

Children, obey your parents in everything, for this is pleasing to the Lord.

Colossians 3:20

. . . humbly regard others as more important than yourselves.

Philippians 2:3

. . . I give thanks to my God through Jesus Christ for all of you . . .

Romans 1:8

Rejoice always.

1 Thessalonians 5:16

Bear one another's burdens, and so you will fulfill the law of Christ.

Galatians 6:2

You are in our hearts.

adapted from 2 Corinthians 7:3

. . . set an example for those who believe, in speech, conduct, love, faith, and purity.

1 Timothy 4:12

God . . . causes the growth.

1 Corinthians 3:7

Gifted with Faith

I have called you by name:
You are mine.
You are precious in my eyes.
I love you.

adapted from Isaiah 43:1,4

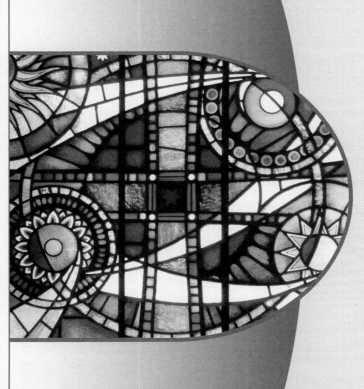

This book belongs to

A Word to the Wise

Put these Scripture verses into your own words.

Turn to me and be safe,
all you ends of the earth,
for I am God; there is
no other!

Isaiah 45:22

_____
_____

He who walks uprightly is
safe, but he whose ways are
crooked falls into the pit.

Proverbs 28:18

_____
_____

A kind mouth multiplies
friends . . .

Sirach 6:5

_____
_____

Do the right and love
goodness, and walk humbly
with your God.

adapted from Micah 6:8

_____
_____

. . . live in a manner
worthy of the call you have
received . . .

Ephesians 4:1

_____
_____

The Name of Jesus

**Color a block every time you use this booklet.
The name of Jesus is a prayer.**

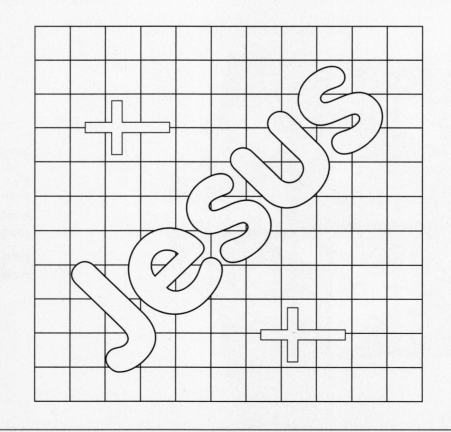

Look at the picture and say "Jesus."

I Ask for Forgiveness

For times . . .

When I did not listen to the Holy Spirit . . .

When I did not pray . . .

When I did not desire forgiveness of sins . . .

When I did not obey . . .

When I hurt others . . .

When I damaged or wasted your gifts . . .

When I was selfish . . .

When I did not say, "I am sorry" for hurting someone's feelings . . .

Jesus, Forgive Me.

You, Lord, who know the hearts of all . . . (Acts of the Apostles 1:24)

Forgive me. Fill me with grace and power.

We Believe

Read the Scripture verses prayerfully. Ask God to help you grow in faith and belief in him.

The kingdom of God is at hand. Repent, and believe in the gospel.

Mark 1:15

I do believe, help my unbelief!

Mark 9:24

Do not be afraid; just have faith.

Mark 5:36

Everyone who believes in Jesus will have eternal life.

adapted from John 3:16

Everything is possible to one who has faith.

Mark 9:23

All who believed were together and had all things in common . . .

Acts of the Apostles 2:44

Pray the psalms—prayers Jesus prayed.

Psalm 62:2–3

My soul rests in God alone,
from whom comes my salvation.
God alone is my rock and salvation,
my secure height; I shall never fall.

Psalm 18:2–4

I love you, LORD, my strength,
LORD, my rock, my fortress, my deliverer,
My God, my rock of refuge,
my shield, . . . my stronghold!
Praised be the LORD, I exclaim!

Psalm 40:2–4

I waited, waited for the LORD;
who bent down and heard my cry,
Drew me . . . out of the mud of the swamp.
Set my feet upon rock . . .
And put a new song in my mouth,
a hymn to our God.
Many shall look on in awe
and they shall trust in the LORD.

Draw what these Scripture verses mean to you.

"I am the light of the world. Whoever follows me will not walk in darkness . . ."   John 8:12

" . . . prepare the way of the LORD!"   Isaiah 40:3

Pray for Others

Write under each host the name of a person for whom you want to pray. When you do pray for that person, color the cross on the host.

. . . love one another as I love you.

John 15:12

" . . . do not worry about your life and what you will eat, or about your body and what you will wear." Luke 12:22

" . . . I have enjoyed God's help to this very day . . . "

Acts of the Apostles 26:22

Prayers Borrowed from Scripture

Write when you might use these prayers.

"My Lord and my God!"
John 20:28

_____

"Lord, save me!"
Matthew 14:30

_____

"Master, we have worked hard all night and have caught nothing, but at your command I will lower the nets."
Luke 5:5

_____

"If you wish, you can make me clean."
Mark 1:40

_____

"Lord, please let me see."
Luke 18:41

_____

"My soul proclaims the greatness of the Lord . . . "
Luke 1:46

_____

"Lord, do not trouble yourself, for I am not worthy to have you enter under my roof . . . but say the word and let my servant be healed."
Luke 7:6,7

_____